Utilize este código QR para se cadastrar de forma mais rápida:

Ou, se preferir, entre em:
www.richmond.com.br/ac/livroportal
e siga as instruções para ter acesso aos conteúdos exclusivos do

Portal e Livro Digital

CÓDIGO DE ACESSO:

A 00062 MAKERS 1 87069

Faça apenas um cadastro. Ele será válido para:

MODERNA Richmond SANTILLANA ESPAÑOL

12111823 Makers 1

Da semente ao livro,
sustentabilidade por todo o caminho

Plantar florestas
A madeira que serve de matéria-prima para nosso papel vem de plantio renovável, ou seja, não é fruto de desmatamento. Essa prática gera milhares de empregos para agricultores e ajuda a recuperar áreas ambientais degradadas.

Fabricar papel e imprimir livros
Toda a cadeia produtiva do papel, desde a produção de celulose até a encadernação do livro, é certificada, cumprindo padrões internacionais de processamento sustentável e boas práticas ambientais.

Criar conteúdos
Os profissionais envolvidos na elaboração de nossas soluções educacionais buscam uma educação para a vida pautada por curadoria editorial, diversidade de olhares e responsabilidade socioambiental.

Taciro Comunicação, Alexandre Santana e Estúdio Pingado

Construir projetos de vida
Oferecer uma solução educacional Moderna é um ato de comprometimento com o futuro das novas gerações, possibilitando uma relação de parceria entre escolas e famílias na missão de educar!

MODERNA

Apoio: TWO SIDES www.twosides.org.br

Fotografe o Código QR e conheça melhor esse caminho. Saiba mais em *moderna.com.br/sustentavel*

#MAKERS 1

ENGLISH ON THE MOVE

STUDENT'S BOOK

SERIES EDITOR:
IZAURA VALVERDE

Richmond

Richmond

Publishing Director: Sandra Possas

Editorial Manager: Izaura Valverde
Digital Content Manager: Adriana Pedro de Almeida

Design Coordinator: Raquel Buim

Senior Editors: Carina Guiname Shiroma, Giuliana Gramani
Editor: Lívia Mantovani
Assistant Editors: Ana Carolina de Castro Gasonato, Beatriz Simões, Leila Scatena, Sheila Folgueral
Digital Content Editors: Ana Paula Campos, Cíntia Afarelli, Gabrielle Navarro, Priscila Oliveira Vieira, Thaís Tardivo
Contents: Camila Vilar, Carina Guiname Shiroma, Erika Thomei Magnoli, Julio Menochelli, Luciana Ananias Maia, Márcia Nogueira, Marise Loureiro, Maya Orsi, Paulo Victor Dantas, Sandra Romani, Vinicius Nobre
Copy Editors: Beatriz Simões, Luisa Soler, Roberta Moratto Risther
Proofreaders: Amanda Moura, Ana Curci, Ana Okada, Barbara Lemos, Carolina Waideman, Danielle Carvalho, Fernanda Bincoletto, Flora Vaz Manzione, Gislaine Caprioli, Katia Vitale, Marina Andrade, Melissa Rodriguez, Patrice Titterington, Rafael Gustavo Spigel, Raura Ikeda, Rich Rafterman, Vivian Cristina

Audio Production: Eastern Sky Media Services

Project Design: Amanda Miyuki, Rafael Gentile
Designers: Amanda Miyuki, David Urbinatti (Teacher's Guide)
Digital Design Editors: Bruno Tersario, Daniel Favalli, Daniel Palmeira, Daniela Carrete, Eloah Cristina, Frodo Almeida, Mônica Oldrine, Roberto Ono
Digital Platform Development: Argeu Pereira da Ivenção (Technology Manager); Luiz Eduardo Mendes Duque (Technology Coordinator); Andrea Carina Pilipposian (Project Supervisor); Carolina Figueiredo (Project Analyst); Ana Paula Campos, Daniela Carrete, Eloah Cristina, Frodo Almeida (Concept Editors)
Educational Portal Content Editor: Sheila Rizzi
Layout: Casa de Ideias
Cover Design: Amanda Savoini
Cover Photos: VladimirFLoyd/iStockphoto, Talaj/iStockphoto, gremlin/iStockphoto, clu/iStockphoto, dolgachov/iStockphoto
Artwork: Amanda Miyuki, Amanda Savoini, Diego Lima, Karina de Sá, Manuel Miramontes, Rafael Gentile
Illustrations: Jorge Pepelife, Leo Gibran
Photo Researchers: Ellen Silvestre, Sara Alencar

Websites mentioned in this material were quoted for didactic purposes only. Richmond has no control over their content and urges care when using them.

Every effort has been made to trace the copyright holders, but if any omission can be rectified, the publishers will be pleased to make the necessary arrangements.

Impressão e acabamento: EGB Editora Gráfica Bernardi Ltda.
Lote: 284492

Dados Internacionais de Catalogação na Publicação (CIP)
(Câmara Brasileira do Livro, SP, Brasil)

#Makers : English on the move / editora responsável Izaura Valverde ; obra coletiva concebida, desenvolvida e produzida pela Editora Moderna. — 1. ed. — São Paulo : Moderna, 2018.

Obra em 4 v. para alunos do 6º ao 9º ano.

1. Inglês (Ensino fundamental) I. Valverde, Izaura.

18-16595 CDD-372.652

Índices para catálogo sistemático:
1. Inglês : Ensino fundamental 372.652
Iolanda Rodrigues Biode - Bibliotecária - CRB-8/10014

ISBN 978-85-16-11182-3 (LA)
ISBN 978-85-16-11183-0 (LP)

Richmond
Editora Moderna Ltda.
Rua Padre Adelino, 758 — Belenzinho
São Paulo — SP — Brasil — CEP 03303-904
www.richmond.com.br
2019
Printed in Brazil

Photos: p. 10: Marko Skrbic/iStockphoto; p. 12: VladimirFLoyd/iStockphoto, Talaj/iStockphoto, gremlin/iStockphoto, clu/iStockphoto, Juanmonino/iStockphoto, kate_sept2004/iStockphoto, gradyreese/iStockphoto, imtmphoto/iStockphoto, djedzura/iStockphoto; p. 13: the8monkey/iStockphoto, monkeybusinessimages/iStockphoto, aldomurillo/iStockphoto; p. 14: KristinaVelickovic/iStockphoto, Poligrafistka/iStockphoto, 221A/iStockphoto, Ismailciydem/iStockphoto, flowgraph/iStockphoto, Ismailciydem/iStockphoto, 221A/iStockphoto, AndrewLinscott/iStockphoto, alexsl/iStockphoto, Nikola93/iStockphoto, izusek/iStockphoto; p. 15: FatCamera/iStockphoto, spfoto/iStockphoto; p. 16: AzmanL/iStockphoto, HAKINMHAN/iStockphoto, leekhoailang/iStockphoto; p. 17: diatrezor/iStockphoto, Baks/iStockphoto, diego_cervo/iStockphoto, AndreyPopov/iStockphoto, AntonioGuillem/iStockphoto, AntonioGuillem/iStockphoto, iStockphoto, byakkaya/iStockphoto, ottoyu/iStockphoto; p. 19: Rawpixel.com/Shutterstock, xavierarnau/iStockphoto, digitalskillet/iStockphoto, kali9/iStockphoto; p. 20: FingerMedium/iStockphoto; p. 21: smodj/iStockphoto, ImageGap/iStockphoto, SweetBabeeJay/iStockphoto, Bennian/Shutterstock, hanohiki/iStockphoto, NeonJellyfish/iStockphoto, PhotographyFirm/iStockphoto; p. 22: serts/iStockphoto; p. 24: laflor/iStockphoto, GeorgeRudy/iStockphoto, lisegagne/iStockphoto, Halfpoint/iStockphoto, Africa Studio/iStockphoto; p. 25: gradyreese/iStockphoto, monkeybusinessimages/iStockphoto, Qvasimodo/iStockphoto; p. 26: Martinan/iStockphoto, Realstock/Shutterstock, Tempura/iStockphoto, SolStock/iStockphoto, Yobro10/iStockphoto; p. 27: wundervisuals/iStockphoto, Wavebreakmedia/iStockphoto, Weekend Images Inc./iStockphoto, mixetto/iStockphoto; p. 28: Nikada/iStockphoto, monkeybusinessimages/iStockphoto, DNF-Style/iStockphoto, OJO Images/Tom Merton/Getty Images; p. 29: matka_Wariatka/iStockphoto, vadimguzhva/iStockphoto, Halfpoint/iStockphoto; p. 31: Imgorthand/iStockphoto, skynesher/iStockphoto, Maica/iStockphoto, SolStock/iStockphoto; p. 33: Everett Collection/Shutterstock; p. 34: 20th Century Fox Television / Alamy / Fotoarena, Disney/Pixar/Alamy/ Fotoarena, Album/Album Cinema/Latinstock, NG Collection/Interfoto/Latinstock, Alamy/Fotoarena; p. 35: spfoto/iStockphoto, ablokhin/iStockphoto, yanikap/iStockphoto, TheDogPhotographer/iStockphoto, IP Galanternik D.U./iStockphoto; p. 36: mgkaya/iStockphoto; p. 38: monkeybusinessimages/iStockphoto, RichLegg/iStockphoto, mediaphotos/iStockphoto, Thanat Jirapongsit/Shutterstock, JodiJacobson/iStockphoto; p. 39: Faysal Ahamed/iStockphoto, Marcus Lindstrom/iStockphoto, doodlemachine/iStockphoto, MarinaMays/iStockphoto; p. 40: enigma_images/iStockphoto, Maudib/iStockphoto, fotostorm/iStockphoto, PhotoEstelar/iStockphoto, _human/iStockphoto, Dizzy/iStockphoto, design56/Shutterstock, exopixel/iStockphoto, gerisima/iStockphoto, Baris-Ozer/iStockphoto, studo58/iStockphoto; p. 41: Weekend Images Inc./iStockphoto; p. 42: scanrail/iStockphoto, subtropica/iStockphoto; p. 43: okili77/Shutterstock, shadowalice/Shutterstock, kolae/iStockphoto, hayim.bevz/iStockphoto, furtaev/iStockphoto; p. 45: Alfa Studio/iStockphoto, Sadeugra/iStockphoto, BHFoton/iStockphoto, petekarici/iStockphoto, Ridofranz/iStockphoto, Yurdakul/iStockphoto, Mosutatsu/iStockphoto, jhorrocks/iStockphoto, HannamariaH/iStockphoto, aekikuis/iStockphoto; p. 47: Carlos Perez, Meriem Mghazli; p. 48: valigursky/iStockphoto; p. 50: Akabei/iStockphoto, georgeclerk/iStockphoto, Davel5957/iStockphoto, YvanDube/iStockphoto, coryz/iStockphoto; p. 51: Color_life/iStockphoto, Weekend Images Inc./iStockphoto, CandO_Designs/iStockphoto, subarashii21/iStockphoto; p. 54: ©2010 GCE Inc. / Dist. by Andrews McMeel Syndication, KellyISP/iStockphoto, PARAMOUNT PICTURES/Album/Fotoarena, Alexlukin/iStockphoto, onurdongel/iStockphoto; p. 55: DanielBendjy/iStockphoto, SIphotography/iStockphoto, nycshooter/iStockphoto, kdshutterman/iStockphoto; p. 56: vgajic/iStockphoto, SIphotography/iStockphoto, Steve Debenport/iStockphoto, monkeybusinessimages/iStockphoto, skynesher/iStockphoto, seb_ra/iStockphoto, Renphoto/iStockphoto; p. 57: andresr/iStockphoto, FatCamera/iStockphoto, somethingway/iStockphoto, Barcin/iStockphoto, Image Source/iStockphoto, monkeybusinessimages/iStockphoto; p. 59: Physicx/iStockphoto; p. 60: ufokim/iStockphoto, BanarTABS/iStockphoto, ChristopherBernard/iStockphoto, cokada/iStockphoto, wsfurlan/iStockphoto, Jevtic/iStockphoto, aldegonde/Shutterstock, buzbuzzer/iStockphoto; p. 61: Aleksandra Zlatkovic/iStockphoto, Bulgac/iStockphoto, ozgurcoskun/iStockphoto, piovesempre/iStockphoto, bgwalker/iStockphoto, atiatiati/iStockphoto; p. 62: pxel66/iStockphoto; p. 64: bowdenimages/iStockphoto, monkeybusinessimages/iStockphoto, Chris Ryan/iStockphoto, damircudic/iStockphoto, monkeybusinessimages/iStockphoto, DragonImages/iStockphoto, dolgachov/iStockphoto; p. 66: STEEX/iStockphoto, harleebob/iStockphoto, gradyreese/iStockphoto, Wavebreakmedia/iStockphoto; p. 67: bigstevemac/iStockphoto, baona/iStockphoto, skynesher/iStockphoto, PeopleImages/iStockphoto; p. 68: chendongshan/iStockphoto, AnnaPustynnikova/iStockphoto, Lecic/iStockphoto; p. 69: kate_sept2004/iStockphoto; p. 70: gradyreese/iStockphoto, Imgorthand/iStockphoto, mediaphotos/iStockphoto, Bigandt_Photography/iStockphoto; p. 71: FGorgun/iStockphoto, 3sbworld/iStockphoto, PeopleImages/iStockphoto, monkeybusinessimages/iStockphoto; p. 73: Laurence Dutton/iStockphoto; p. 74: courtneyk/iStockphoto; p. 76: Jon Bilous/Shutterstock, De Jongh Photography/Shutterstock, Nicola Ferrari/iStockphoto, RaksyBH/Shutterstock, Val Thoermer/Shutterstock; p. 77: STEEX/iStockphoto, monkeybusinessimages/iStockphoto, Juanmonino/iStockphoto; p. 78: AlexKozlov/iStockphoto, kozmoat98/iStockphoto, AlbertPego/iStockphoto, browndogstudios/iStockphoto, appleuzr/iStockphoto, -VICTOR-/iStockphoto; p. 79: Si-Gal/iStockphoto; p. 80: Feifei Cui-Paoluzzo/Getty Images, Clarence Holmes Photography / Alamy / Fotoarena, steverts/iStockphoto, Lya_Cattel/iStockphoto, Holly Vegter/Shutterstock, Roberto Herrett/Alamy/Fotoarena; p. 81: Starcevic/iStockphoto, franckreporter/iStockphoto, typhoonski/iStockphoto, User10095428_393/iStockphoto; p. 82: Kingsman Asset/Shutterstock, Maurizio De Mattei/Shutterstock, LizzieMaher/iStockphoto, Kenishirotie/Shutterstock, Elvinagraph/iStockphoto, nickylarson974/iStockphoto, alessandro0770/iStockphoto, lettett/Shutterstock; p. 83: JackF/iStockphoto, STEEX/iStockphoto, Hero Images/Getty Images, andresr/iStockphoto; p. 85: Pumidol/Shutterstock, paylessimages/iStockphoto, Stefan Laws/iStockphoto, FernandoPodolski/iStockphoto; p. 87: AKKHARAT JARUSILAWONG/Shutterstock, Michael Greenwood/Getty Images, Jon Cartwright/Getty Images, gibgalich/iStockphoto, Infografx/iStockphoto; p. 88: master1305/iStockphoto; p. 91: Juanmonino/iStockphoto, UberImages/iStockphoto, good_reason08/iStockphoto; p. 92: gradyreese/iStockphoto, Wavebreakmedia/iStockphoto, Steve Debenport/iStockphoto, mixetto/iStockphoto, Drazen_/iStockphoto, Annykos/iStockphoto; p. 94: skynesher/iStockphoto, martin-dm/Istockpphoto; p. 95: cferrin/iStockphoto, isitsharp/iStockphoto, YakobchukOlena/iStockphoto, Imgorthand/iStockphoto, jkitan/iStockphoto, Imgorthand/iStockphoto; p. 97: kali9/iStockphoto; p. 99: FOX, DISNEY/BUENA VISTA, ABC, South_agency/iStockphoto, slinscot/iStockphoto, TerryJ/iStockphoto, BBC, DISNEY/BUENA VISTA, Warner Bros.; p. 100: MangoStar_Studio/iStockphoto; p. 102: Georgethefourth/iStockphoto, ssj414/iStockphoto, nicolamargaret/iStockphoto, David Osberg/iStockphoto, MachineHeadz/iStockphoto; p. 103: halfbottle/iStockphoto, bonezboyz/iStockphoto, Good_Studio/iStockphoto; p. 104: somethingway/iStockphoto, RenataOs/Shutterstock, bradleyhebdon/iStockphoto, LSOphoto/iStockphoto, monkeybusinessimages/iStockphoto, Louis-Paul St-Onge/iStockphoto, D-Keine/iStockphoto, monkeybusinessimages/iStockphoto, Floortje/iStockphoto, Tuanjai/iStockphoto, KucherAV/Shutterstock; p. 105: sureeporn/iStockphoto; p. 106: Image Source/iStockphoto; p. 107: ActionPics/iStockphoto, CDH_Design/iStockphoto, simonkr/iStockphoto; p. 109: michaelmurillo/iStockphoto, mauinow1/iStockphoto, artisteer/iStockphoto, Anton Violin/Shutterstock, Pongasn68/iStockphoto; p. 111: Rafael Mantesso; p. 112: South_agency/iStockphoto, PeopleImages/iStockphoto, mladn61/iStockphoto, Coral222/iStockphoto, zeljkosantrac/iStockphoto, tommaso79/iStockphoto, Wavebreakmedia/iStockphoto; p. 114: Floortje/iStockphoto, zcw/iStockphoto, Floortje/iStockphoto, Bedrin-Alexander/iStockphoto, IsraelMckee/iStockphoto; p. 115: Saracin/iStockphoto, PrasongTakham/iStockphoto, mamophoto/iStockphoto, Molnia/iStockphoto; p. 116: vladru/iStockphoto, Sergey Peterman/iStockphoto, kyoshino/iStockphoto, Floortje/iStockphoto, Irina Nartova/Shutterstock; p. 117: malerapaso/iStockphoto, Floortje/iStockphoto, kev303/iStockphoto, subjug/iStockphoto, chairboy/iStockphoto; p. 118: golero/iStockphoto; p. 119: MaskaRad/iStockphoto, real444/iStockphoto, fbxx/iStockphoto, deepblue4you/iStockphoto; p. 121: Dibettadifino/iStockphoto, danielvfung/iStockphoto; p. 122: seb_ra/iStockphoto, NoDerog/iStockphoto, sorendls/iStockphoto, smiltena/iStockphoto; p. 124: PeopleImages/iStockphoto, LightFieldStudios/iStockphoto; p. 126: kulkann/iStockphoto, Frank and Helena/iStockphoto, Imgorthand/iStockphoto, mixetto/iStockphoto, Choreograph/iStockphoto; p. 127: monkeybusinessimages/iStockphoto, petrograd99/iStockphoto, kali9/iStockphoto, Milkos/iStockphoto, MicrovOne/iStockphoto; p. 128: martin-dm/iStockphoto, Wavebreakmedia/iStockphoto, Avosb/iStockphoto; p. 130: santypan/iStockphoto; p. 132: trinetuzun/iStockphoto, Delpixart/iStockphoto, Trinet Uzun/Shutterstock, trinetuzun/iStockphoto; p. 133: marcoventuriniautieri/iStockphoto, peeterv/iStockphoto, justhavealook/iStockphoto; p. 137: monkeybusinessimages/iStockphoto; p. 138: Electra-K-Vasileiadou/iStockphoto; p. 139: oxygen_8/iStockphoto, monkeybusinessimages/iStockphoto, Alexa-Mitiner/iStockphoto; p. 140: BrianAJackson/iStockphoto, gradyreese/iStockphoto, PeopleImages/iStockphoto, monkeybusinessimages/iStockphoto, gorodenkoff/iStockphoto, lushik/iStockphoto, LueratSatichob/iStockphoto, AVIcons/iStockphoto, Amin Yusifov/iStockphoto, lushik/iStockphoto; p. 141: Floortje/iStockphoto, PetrMalyshev/iStockphoto, Floortje/iStockphoto, kyoshino/iStockphoto, luismmolina/iStockphoto, alex_kz/iStockphoto, Sladic/iStockphoto, woolzian/iStockphoto, klenova/iStockphoto; p. 142: IconicBestiary/iStockphoto, dark_ink/iStockphoto, DRogatnev/Shutterstock, Artisticco/Shutterstock, artisticco/iStockphoto, DRogatnev/Shutterstock, MarianVejcik/iStockphoto; p. 143: ©1969 Peanuts Worldwide LLC. / Dist. by Andrews McMeel Syndication, doodlemachine/iStockphoto, Paul Bradbury/iStockphoto, Mikolette/iStockphoto, warrengoldswain/iStockphoto, eli_asenova/iStockphoto, lovro77/iStockphoto, ByeByeTokyo/iStockphoto; p. 144: Kuzmichstudio/iStockphoto, shironosov/iStockphoto, Sam Edwards/iStockphoto, CBCK-Christine/iStockphoto, Weekend Images Inc./iStockphoto, Alamy/Fotoarena; p. 145: Ilyabolotov/iStockphoto, Yuzach/iStockphoto, adekvat/iStockphoto; p. 146: monkeybusinessimages/iStockphoto, Artfoliophoto/iStockphoto, monkeybusinessimages/iStockphoto, AndreyPopov/iStockphoto, RichVintage/iStockphoto, yanjf/iStockphoto, mixetto/iStockphoto; p. 147: A Sharma/Shutterstock; p. 148: NadyaRa/Shutterstock, EddieHernandezPhotography/iStockphoto; p. 149: Fnsy/iStockphoto, Steve Debenport/iStockphoto; p. 151: Thurtell/iStockphoto

CONTENTS

SCOPE AND SEQUENCE

Listening	Speaking	Reading	Writing	Pronunciation
• Two preteens introducing themselves	• Introducing yourself	• Social media profile	• Social media profile	• /m/
• A preteen introducing her family	• Presentation of your family	• Photo captions	• Photo caption	• /ð/
• School tour	• Podcast presenting your school	• School posters	• Poster	• /θ/
• Bedroom tour	• Bedroom tour	• Comic strip	• Alternate ending for a comic strip	• Stress in compound nouns
• A surprise for a friend	• Surprise for a friend	• Chat	• Chat messages	• /ŋ/
• Neighborhood descriptions	• Presentation about your neighborhood	• Street signs	• Sign for school	• /n/
• Interview about free-time activities	• Interview about free-time activities	• Blog post	• Blog post	• /t/ vs. /tʃ/
• Description of a routine	• Description of your routine	• Weekly schedule	• Weekly schedule	• *-s* in 3rd person singular verbs

BATHROOM
Good morning.
I'm Mr. ________.
What's your name?
I'm Lucy
____

WELCOME

1 Find 8 hidden letters in the doodle and color them. Then write a word you know in English that starts with each of these letters.

T- Tokio　　A- Anny　　E - elefant　　P - pig

M- mom　　S- snake　　C- cow　　K- Katize

2 Draw the other letters of the alphabet in the doodle. How many words can you form using only those letters?

book, desk, fget, good, hour, indian, jar, lion, near, open, queen, rigt, union, very, X-man, zebra

3 Follow the instructions. Then work in pairs and practice the dialogue.

1 Invent a last name for the teacher and complete his speech bubble.

2 Invent a last name for the student and complete her speech bubble.

3 Follow the model below and take turns spelling their names.

A: What's the teacher's/student's last name?

B: It's Oshiro.

A: How do you spell it?

B: O – S – H – I – R – O.

4 Draw yourself on the desk next to the girl. Then draw a speech bubble and write your answer to the teacher.

5 Read the teacher's speech bubble again and underline the greeting he uses. What other greetings do you use to...

START A CONVERSATION?

Hi! Hello!
How are you?
Good morning!
Good afternoon!

END A CONVERSATION?

Bye!
Bye - bye!
See you later!
Good night!
See you!

6 Find the following items in the doodle and match them to the colors from the box.

black blue brown gray
green orange pink
purple red white yellow

1 apple ____________
2 bike ____________
3 cat ____________
4 dog ____________
5 flower ____________
6 moon ____________
7 pencil ____________
8 robot ____________
9 star ____________
10 table ____________
11 vase ____________

7 Find 2 items that start with the same letter as each of the elements in activity 6. Then paint them according to the color code from the previous activity.

8 🎧 2 Listen and complete the sentences with the numbers spelled out. Then write the numbers in the doodle.

1 I have ____________ dollars in my wallet.
2 The speed limit is ____________ kilometers per hour.
3 My address is ____________ Beale Street.
4 It's ____________ in the afternoon now.
5 Let's go. We can take the ____________ bus.
6 The teddy bear costs ____________ dollars and ____________ cents.

9 Answer the question using a complete sentence and draw the candles on the birthday cake.

A: How old are you?

B: ________________________________

10 Make a doodle or a collage of images with all the numbers you see around you. Share it on #MAKERS Digital <www.richmondmakers.com>. Use the hashtag #NumbersAroundMe.

11 Look for the missing words in the doodle and complete the questions.

1 How do you say *domingo* in ____________?
2 May I go to the ____________?
3 Can you ____________, please?

12 Write the sentences from the box in the corresponding speech bubble.

Can I come in?
I don't understand.
What's the meaning of "garden"?

13 What other questions or sentences are useful to you in class?

1

ABOUT ME

OBJECTIVES

- Introduce oneself.
- Talk about countries and nationalities.
- Identify the months of the year.
- Identify the characteristics of a social media profile and understand its purpose.
- Use the verb to be to describe a state or a characteristic.
- Write a social media profile.
- Investigate the English words students use in their everyday lives.
- Reflect about how and why English is used in local businesses in different countries.
- Give opinions about having friends who are too similar to oneself.

Read the questions and discuss.

1 What can you see in the image?
2 How old are you?
3 Do you like being your age?
4 What's it like being your age?

Richmond

#MAKERS DIGITAL

1 Martin

2 Sharon

3 Jamila

4 Steve

5 Diana

RTV

1 Look at the images. How old do you think the preteens are?

2 Check the topics you think the preteens will mention when talking about themselves.

		Your Predictions	Topics Mentioned
a	body changes		
b	chores		
c	family		
d	food		
e	friends		
f	internet		
g	pets		
h	place of origin		
i	school		
j	teachers		

3 🎧 3 Listen to the preteens talking about themselves. Then check the topics they mention in the chart in activity 2.

4 🎧 4 Who said it? Listen again and write the name of the person next to each sentence.

1 I have to take care of my brother and feed my dog. __________

2 It's my birthday today. __________

3 I'm not a child anymore, but I'm still not a teenager. __________

4 My parents let me go out with my friends by myself. __________

5 I'm biracial and I spend a lot of time with my friends. __________

React!

5 Write a comment about the audio.

X gamer I'm biracial too. I have a Japanese-Peruvian dad and a French-Canadian mom.

2 weeks ago — 1 Great! Reply

Pablo Sanches Being 11 is awesome… Good times!

3 months ago — Great! Reply

Abby Brown So real and honest… These kids are the best! :)

6 months ago — Great! Reply

____

POST

I Wonder

6 Write a question about students from other countries that are your age. Then look for the answer.

____

99 Great! 99 Interact

LANGUAGE 1

1 Read the sentences and answer the questions.

I am **American**.

My mom's from **Haiti** and my father is from **Nigeria**.

1 Which words refer to countries?

____

2 Which words refer to nationalities?

____

2 Complete the chart with the corresponding countries or nationalities. Use the dictionary to help you.

		Country	Nationality
1		Australia	Australian
2			Brazilian
3		England	
4		Germany	
5			Haitian
6		India	
7	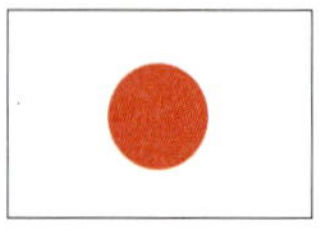	Japan	
8			Nigerian
9		Scotland	
10		The United States	

Snack Learning

Capital Letters

Haiti

American

3 5 Listen to Amelia talking about her classmates and complete the sentences with their nationalities.

1 Yoko is _______________.

2 Luca is _______________.

3 Lilly is _______________.

4 Stanley is _______________.

5 Ginny is _______________.

6 Chidi is _______________.

4 Write the country of origin of each cultural element.

1 Sushi is from _______________.

2 Koalas are from _______________.

3 Schnitzel is from _______________.

4 The New York Yankees are from _______________.

5 Harry Potter is from _______________.

My Glossary

5 Complete the sentences with information about you.

1 My name's _______________ and I'm from _______________.

2 My favorite singer is _______________. He's/She's _______________.

3 My favorite food is _______________. It's from _______________.

4 My favorite athlete is _______________. He's/She's from _______________.

Study Space

LISTING AND SPEAKING

1 🎧 6 **Listen to a boy and a girl introducing themselves. Then complete the forms.**

1
NAME Primrose
NICKNAME Prim
AGE ______ years old
NATIONALITY

2
NAME Samuel
NICKNAME
AGE ______ years old
NATIONALITY

2 🎧 7 **Listen again and write P (Primrose) or S (Samuel).**

1 ☐ My favorite color is yellow.
2 ☐ I love soccer.
3 ☐ I have two dogs: Rocky and Bella.
4 ☐ My favorite kind of food is Japanese.
5 ☐ I have three sisters.
6 ☐ I love gymnastics.

Study Space

Buzzwords

*"I love gymnastics. It's, **like**, so much fun!"*

What does "like" mean in this context? Look it up!

Pronunciation

3 **Are there words ending in *m* in your language? If so, how is the *m* pronounced?**

4 🎧 8 **Listen to Primrose and Samuel again and notice how they pronounce the words in bold. Is it similar to how words ending in *m* are pronounced in your language?**

I'm Prim and **I'm from** the United States.

I'm Sam and **I'm** on the soccer **team**.

5 🎧 9 **Listen again and practice the sentences from activity 4.**

6 **Plan a short video to introduce yourself.**

Hi, everyone! I'm ____________, but my friends call me ____________. I'm ____________ years old and I'm from ____________. This is my first video on this channel. Here are three facts about me.

- **Fact number 1:** my favorite ____________ is ____________.
- **Fact number 2:** I have ____________.
- **Fact number 3:** I love ____________.

Thank you so much for watching! Bye!

7 **Record your video and share it on #MAKERS Digital <www.richmondmakers.com>. Use the hashtag #IntroducingMyself.**

READING

Before Reading

1 Look at the text and underline the correct options.

1 We can find this text **in a book** / **on the internet**.

2 This text is a **social media profile** / **blog**.

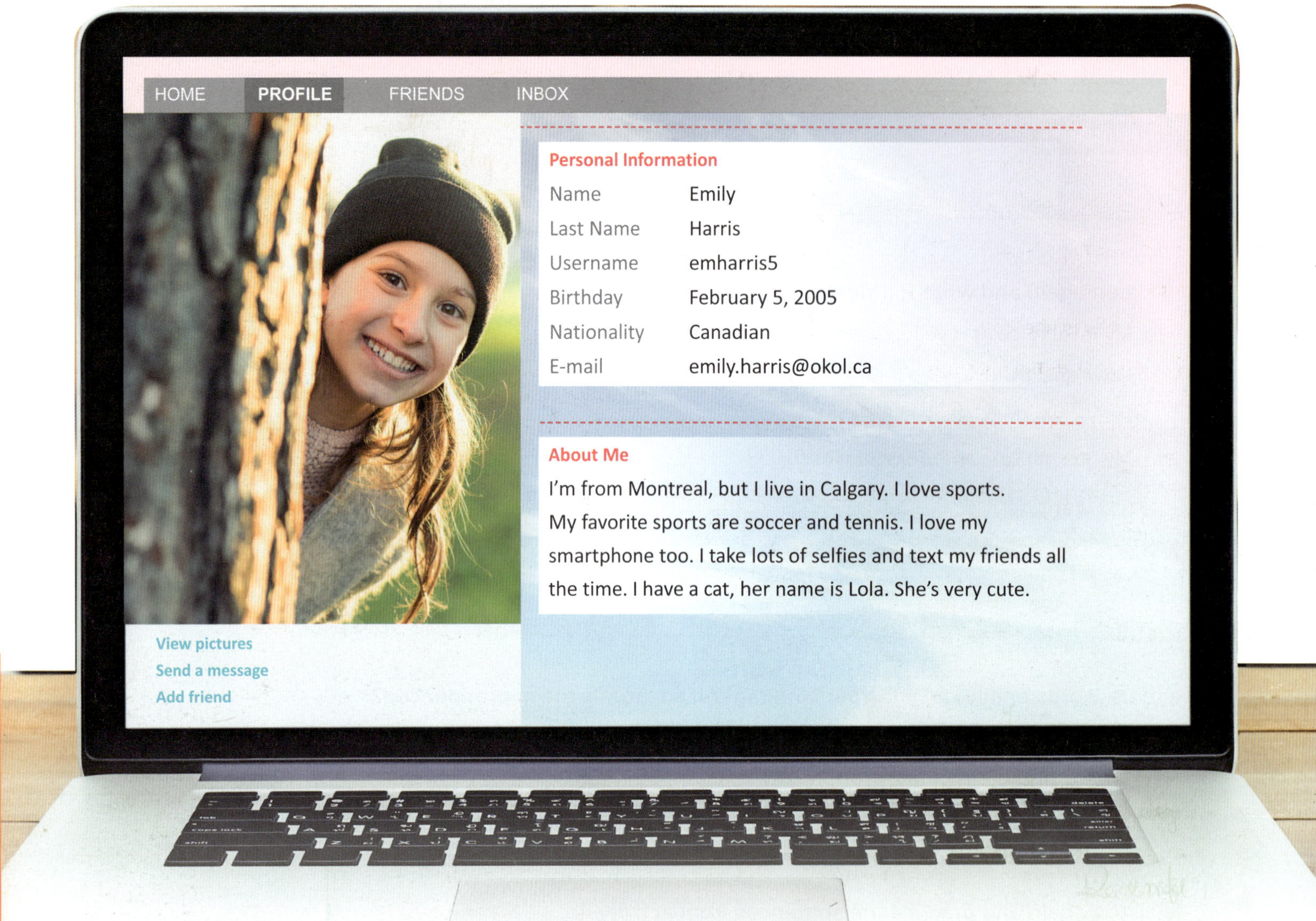

2 Look at the text and check the correct answers.

1 People complete this text to...
- a ☐ give information about themselves.
- b ☐ buy a product.

2 This text...
- a ☐ contains titles and fields.
- b ☐ presents people's personal information.
- c ☐ is a fictional text.
- d ☐ usually contains a picture.

3 The author of this text is...
- a ☐ Lola.
- b ☐ Emily.
- c ☐ a professional writer.

4 This text can be found...
- a ☐ in academic books.
- b ☐ on sticky notes.
- c ☐ on social media.

While Reading

3 **Read Emily's profile and write T (true) or F (false). Then correct the false statements.**

1 [F] Emily is Scottish.
Emily is Canadian

2 [T] Her username is emharris5.

3 [F] Her birthday is in January.
Her birthday is in February

4 [T] She loves sports.

4 **Read the text again and answer the questions.**

1 What is Emily's last name? Harris
2 How old is she? 16 years old
3 Which city is she from? Montreal
4 What is her e-mail? emily.harris@chd.ca

5 **Check the correct answers.**

1 What are Emily's favorite sports?

a [ ]

b [X]

c [X]

2 What does Emily use her smartphone for?

a [X]

b [ ]

c [X]

3 What pet does Emily have?

a [ ]

b [ ]

c [X]

Study Space

After Reading

6 **Would you be friends with Emily? Why?**

Workbook p. 137

LANGUAGE 2

1 **What is Emily saying? Complete the sentences. Then underline the verbs.**

2 **Read the sentences in activity 1 and check the correct options.**

The verb to be comes after...

a ☐ a personal pronoun.
b ☐ an adjective.
c ☐ a singular noun.
d ☐ a plural noun.

Verb to Be

I	**am**	11 years old.
You	**are**	my friend.
He	**is**	a student.
She	**is**	happy.
It	**is**	a cat.
We	**are**	students.
You	**are**	Brazilian.
They	**are**	from the U.S.

The verb to be is used to **describe a state or a characteristic.**

Snack Learning

Months of the Year

January	May	September
February	June	October
March	July	November
April	August	December

3 **Check the correct option to complete the sentences.**

1 Spencer ________ 12 years old.
a ☐ am b ☐ is c ☐ are

2 You and your friend ________ very beautiful!
a ☐ am b ☐ is c ☐ are

3 I ________ from Nigeria.
a ☐ am b ☐ is c ☐ are

4 I have a dog. His name ________ Thor.
a ☐ am b ☐ is c ☐ are

5 Fred and George ________ twin brothers.
a ☐ am b ☐ is c ☐ are

6 Carol and I ________ best friends.
a ☐ am b ☐ is c ☐ are

7 Lisbon ________ a beautiful city.
a ☐ am b ☐ is c ☐ are

8 I ________ Harry's sister.
a ☐ am b ☐ is c ☐ are

9 My brother and my sister ________ happy today.
a ☐ am b ☐ is c ☐ are

10 This is Lucas and I ________ Kathy.
a ☐ am b ☐ is c ☐ are

4 **Write the correct month of the year.**

1 New Year's Day is in ________.
2 Mother's Day is in ________.
3 Summer vacation begins in ________.
4 My birthday is in ________.
5 My best friend's birthday is in ________.

Snack Learning

Contractions

I am = I'm
You are = You're
He is = He's
She is = She's
It is = It's
We are = We're
You are = You're
They are = They're

5 Complete the dialogue between the students with the contracted form of the verb to be.

Carol: Hi! You (1) ______ the new student, right?

Dylan: Right. My name (2) ______ Dylan. I (3) ______ Australian.

Laura: Hey, Dylan! We (4) ______ Laura and Carol.

Dylan: Hey there! But who (5) ______ who?

Laura: I (6) ______ Laura. And she (7) ______ Carol, of course!

Carol: Come and meet some of our friends.

Dylan: Sure!

Laura: Dylan, these are Gabe and his sister Emma. They (8) ______ English.

Dylan: Hi, everyone!

Gabe: Welcome to our school!

Emma: Hurry up! We (9) ______ late for class.

6 Read the text and complete it with *am*, *is* or *are*.

Hello! I (1) ______ James. I (2) ______ English. I (3) ______ 14 years old and my birthday (4) ______ in October. My e-mail (5) ______ james13@pezzmail.com. My favorite colors (6) ______ blue and green. My favorite sport (7) ______ basketball.

These (8) ______ my sisters. Ava and Mia (9) ______ twins. They (10) ______ 6 years old and their birthday (11) ______ in July. Their favorite color (12) ______ red.

This (13) ______ Oliver. He (14) ______ 13 years old and he (15) ______ American. Oliver and I (16) ______ best friends. We love video games. Our favorite games (17) ______ Super Mario Bros. and Minecraft.

7 Talk about yourself. Mention the topics below.

- name
- nationality
- age
- your birthday
- your e-mail
- your favorite color(s) and game(s)

Study Space

Workbook p. 137

WRITING

My Social Media Profile

Before Writing

1 **Plan your profile.**

- What information do you want to include in your profile?
- Do you prefer to use a picture of yourself or an avatar? Why?

Drafting

2 **Write your personal information and a draft of the About Me section.**

Personal Information

I'm 11 years old, I like hamburguer and pizza I don't it like manga, I have a dog, his name is Scooby My favorite color is black and white. My name is Itala

About Me

3 **Share your social media profile with a classmate and ask for his/her opinion. Make adjustments, if necessary.**

Final Writing

4 **Write the final version of your profile and publish it on #MAKERS Digital <www.richmondmakers.com>. Use the hashtag #MyProfile.**

INVESTIGATE

few some a lot of

I use _some_ words in English in my everyday life.

Collect Data

- For three days, make a list of the words in English you use.
- Divide the words in your list into two categories: words you use when talking and words you use when writing.

Words Used When Talking	Words Used When Writing
top	show
show	brother
boy	top

- Make sure you list the words you use in conversations, texts to friends, posts online, entries in your diary etc.

Analyze the Data

- How many words in English are there in your list?
- Do you use more words in English when talking or when writing?
- Which words in your list do you use more frequently?
- In which context(s) do you use English more frequently?

Draw a Conclusion

I use _some_ words in English in my everyday life.

1 **Reflect on your conclusion and discuss the questions in pairs.**

1 Are you surprised by the result of your investigation? Why?

2 What do you think about the number of words in English you use?

2 **Share your ideas on #MAKERS Digital <www.richmondmakers.com>. Use the hashtag #WordsInEnglish.**

LOCAL AND GLOBAL

1 **Look at the images and discuss the questions with a classmate.**

1

2

3

4

5

6

7

a Which language is present in all the images?

b Which of these words and expressions can you see in your country?

2 **Reflect and take notes.**

1 Which other words in English do you see or hear frequently?

2 In which other situations are you exposed to English in your daily life?

3 **In which situations does speaking English help people access the information they need? What can you do to improve your access to information in English?**

IMAGINE

Imagine that all your friends are very similar to you.

1 **Read the article. Then discuss the questions with a classmate.**

1 According to the article, what kind of people make best friends? Why?

2 In your opinion, is the information in the article surprising? Why?

RTV

2

WE ARE FAMILY

OBJECTIVES

- Talk about the members of your family and different types of families.
- Identify characteristics of photo captions and understand their purpose.
- Use the verb to be to talk about families.
- Use demonstrative pronouns to talk about things that are close to or far from you.
- Write a photo caption.
- Investigate how many children on average your family members have.
- Reflect on the lives of bilingual people from multicultural families.
- Give opinions about different types of families.

LISTENING AND SPEAKING

1 11 Listen to Lily introducing her family. Which image represents them? Check the correct option.

a 

b 

c 

2 12 Listen to Lily again. Then match the names to the words that describe how they are related to Lily.

1	Jack	a ☐	pet
2	Phil	b ☐	brother
3	Helena	c ☐	mother
4	Vincent	d ☐	grandmother
5	Tina	e ☐	father
6	Bobby	f ☐	grandfather

3 13 Listen one more time and circle the correct options to complete the sentences.

1 Lily has **one brother** / **two brothers**.
2 Jack **dances** / **sings** very well.
3 Her father is **serious** / **funny**.
4 Her mother makes **paintings** / **movies**.
5 Her mother is **funny** / **creative**.
6 Her grandparents are good at telling **jokes** / **stories**.
7 Her **dog** / **cat** is also part of her family.

Buzzwords

*"I like to **hang out** with them because they play games with me."*
What does "hang out" mean in this context? Look it up!

Study Space

4 Plan a presentation about your family.

Hi! I'm ________ and this is my family.
This is my ________. His/Her name is ________. He/She is ________.
____
____
Finally, this is my ________. His/Her name is ________. He/She is ________. Isn't my family great/beautiful/awesome?
I hope you liked my presentation! Bye!

5 Record a video of your presentation and share it on #MAKERS Digital <www.richmondmakers.com>. Use the hashtag #ThisIsMyFamily.

READING

Before Reading

1 **Look at the images and the texts. Then underline the correct options to complete the text below. Sometimes more than one answer is correct.**

This kind of text accompanies a (1) **drawing / picture** and it can come (2) **above / below** it. These texts are normally (3) **short / long** and are called (4) **subtitles / photo captions**.

1

junebarry13

102 likes

junebarry13 This is my dad (and that's our book collection—we love to read!). Aaaaaaaaaaaaand… it's his birthday today! He's 43 now! Happy birthday, @samuelhbarry! 🎉 🎁 🎊 You are an amazing dad who does it all alone! Love our #SmallButGreatFamily #JustTheTwoOfUs

2

Paul Smith

Those are me and Kelly on the background and these are Sophie and Parker with the newest member of our family: Rufus! 🐶 They have asked for a "brother" for so long and now he's here! Are they happy? Of course they are! And Rufus loves to hang out with his new family and we all love him too!

50 Likes 10 Comments

Like Comment Share

3

The Duke and Duchess of Genebraltar present their baby boy, Phillip, to the world in their luxurious house in the capital.

4

This is my family: my mom and dad on top, me on the left, then my little brother, Christopher, and Mikaela, my sister, on the right. Here we are in the park near our house on the day Christopher was adopted. Christopher, Mikaela and I are not our parents' biological children, but the only thing that matters is that we all love each other very much! (Oct. 20, 2018)

While Reading

2 **Look at the images again and read the texts. Which text is published in each of these places?**

a

magazines

b

photo album

c

social media

3 **What is the purpose of this kind of text? Check all the correct answers.**

- a ☐ To describe the image it accompanies.
- b ☐ To leave a comment on somebody else's post.
- c ☐ To identify who is who in an image.
- d ☐ To share an interesting experience with friends.
- e ☐ To give an opinion about a text.

4 **Read the texts again. Then match the people to the information about them.**

1 Philip...

2 Sophie...

3 Christopher...

4 June...

- a ☐ is adopted.
- b ☐ has a new pet.
- c ☐ is still a baby.
- d ☐ is celebrating somebody's birthday.

5 **Look at the hashtags in text 1. What can we infer about June's family? Circle the correct options.**

1 She **is** / **isn't** an only child.

2 She **likes** / **doesn't like** having a small family.

3 She **lives** / **doesn't live** with her mother.

6 **Read text 2 again and check the correct answer.**

1 Who is Rufus?

2 Which element allows the reader to infer that?

- a ☐ The words in the text.
- b ☐ The comments in the text.
- c ☐ The emoji in the text.

3 Why is there an emoji in Paul's text?

- a ☐ To express emotions.
- b ☐ To illustrate his ideas.
- c ☐ To replace words for images.

Study Space

After Reading

7 **Which family is more similar to yours? Why?**

8 **Do you usually write captions for pictures? Why?**

9 **In your opinion, what is the importance of photo captions?**

Workbook p. 139

LANGUAGE 2

1 Read some sentences from the texts on page 28 and write A (affirmative), N (negative) or I (interrogative).

1 [ ] He's 43 now!
2 [ ] You are an amazing dad who does it all alone!
3 [ ] Are they happy?
4 [ ] Christopher, Mikaela and I are not our parents' biological children.

Verb to Be

Negative

I	am not	Italian.
You	**are not/aren't**	my teacher.
He	**is not/isn't**	nine years old.
She	**is not/isn't**	sad.
It	**is not/isn't**	cold today.
We	**are not/aren't**	cousins.
You	**are not/aren't**	from Greece.
They	**are not/aren't**	here.

Interrogative

Am	I	sick?
Are	you	happy?
Is	he	your dad?
Is	she	a student?
Is	it	a cute bunny?
Are	we	late?
Are	you	hungry?
Are	they	Portuguese?

Short Answers

Affirmative	Negative
Yes, I am.	No, I'm not.
Yes, you are.	No, you aren't.
Yes, he is.	No, he isn't.
Yes, she is.	No, she isn't.
Yes, it is.	No, it isn't.
Yes, we are.	No, we aren't.
Yes, you are.	No, you aren't.
Yes, they are.	No, they aren't.

2 Complete the sentences using the verb to be.

1 I ___ a pilot; I'm a nurse.
2 We ___ sisters; she's my cousin.
3 It ___ very cold today, so you don't need to take a jacket.
4 My brother ___ 12 years old; he's 14.
5 You ___ late for class, so you don't need to hurry.
6 My classmate ___ Japanese; he's from China.

3 Complete the sentences using the correct form of the verb to be so that they are true for you.

1 Orange juice ___ my favorite drink.
2 I ___ very good at English.
3 I think fantasy books ___ interesting.
4 My family members ___ very close.
5 It ___ rainy today.

4 Write questions using the prompts and the verb to be.

1 your grandmother / from France
___
2 your Science teacher / Canadian
___
3 you / hungry
___
4 your family / big
___
5 you / an only child
___
6 you / 11 years old
___
7 your parents / Spanish
___

5 Answer the questions in activity 4 about yourself. Use short answers.

1 ___
2 ___
3 ___
4 ___
5 ___
6 ___
7 ___

Study Space

6 Read some sentences from the texts on page 28 and observe the words in bold. Then answer the questions.

1 **This** is my dad...

2 ... **that**'s our book collection...

3 **Those** are me and Kelly on the background...

4 ... **these** are Sophie and Parker...

a In which sentences do the words in bold refer to singular elements? ____

b In which sentences do the words in bold refer to plural elements? ____

c In which sentences do the words in bold refer to elements that are near the speaker? ____

d In which sentences do the words in bold refer to elements that are far from the speaker? ____

Demonstrative Pronouns

This right here is my cousin.
These are my twin brothers: the one on my left is Mark and the one on my right is Tom.
That over there is my house. Can you see it?
Those are my pets running to the garden. They're really fast!

The demonstrative pronouns *this* and *these* are used to refer to **elements that are close to the speaker** (*this* if it is singular or *these* if it is plural). *That* and *those* are used to refer to **elements that are far from the speaker** (*that* if it is singular or *those* if it is plural).

Pronunciation

7 14 Listen to a description of a family picture and notice how the words in bold are pronounced. Is the *th* sound the same in all of them?

This is my **father** and **this** is my **mother**. **That** is my **brother** and **that** over **there** is my **other brother**. **These** are my pets and **those** are **their** toys. **They** love to play **together**.

8 Does your language have the same sound? If not, does it have a similar sound?

9 15 Listen to the description in activity 7 again and practice it.

10 Look at the images and complete the sentences with the correct demonstrative pronoun.

1

I think ____ statues are beautiful.

2

Do you need help with ____ activity?

3

Can you see ____ tall building?

4

____ pictures from the party are my favorite.

Workbook p. 139

WRITING

A Photo Caption

Before Writing

1 Plan your text.

- Which picture are you going to write a caption for?
- Are there people in it? Does the picture show a special place? Are there any relevant objects in it?
- Which information do you want to give about this picture?
- Where do you imagine your picture and its caption would be: on social media, in a photo album, in a magazine or newspaper etc.?
- Which aspects should be present in your text, depending on where you are going to publish it?

Drafting

2 Write a draft of your text.

3 Share your caption with a classmate and ask for his/her opinion. Make adjustments, if necessary.

Final Writing

4 Write the final version of your photo caption and publish it, along with the picture, on #MAKERS Digital <www.richmondmakers.com>. Use the hashtag #MyPhotoCaption.

INVESTIGATE

On average, people in my family have ____________ child/children.

Collect Data

- Talk to the members of your extended family (grandparents, uncles, aunts, cousins etc.). Try to interview as many people as possible. Ask them how many children they have and make a chart.

Family Member	Number of Children

Analyze the Data

- How many children do each of the relatives that you interviewed have?
- Calculate the average number of children your family members have. In order to do that, add the number of children each of them has and divide it by the number of family members you interviewed. For example: if you interview three people and one has two children, the other has one child and the third one has three children, add two, one and three ($2 + 1 + 3 = 6$) and divide it by the number of people interviewed ($6 \div 3 = 2$), so the average is two.

Draw a Conclusion

On average, people in my family have ____________ child/children.

1 Reflect on your conclusion and discuss the following questions.

1. Based on your research, would you define your family as big or small?
2. Do you like having a big/small family? Why?
3. What are the positive and negative aspects of having a big/small family?
4. Can you see any differences in the number of children your grandparents have and the number of children your parents, uncles and aunts have?
5. Do all the couples in your family have children?
6. Are there any single parents in your family?

2 Share your ideas on #MAKERS Digital <www.richmondmakers.com>. Use the hashtag #GenerationsOfMyFamily.

LOCAL AND GLOBAL

1 What language(s) do you speak with your family? Do you use the same language at home and at school?

2 Read the text about Mila Kunis and discuss the questions with a classmate.

Believe it or not, actress Mila Kunis speaks fluent Russian! Mila was born in Ukraine (then USSR) in 1983, so Russian is her native language. In 1991, her family moved to the United States, so Mila continued speaking Russian at home, but spoke English at school and at her drama classes.

1 How do you think it is like to be born in one country and grow up in another one?
2 In your opinion, what are the positive and negative aspects of speaking different languages at home and at school?

3 Research people who grew up in bilingual environments. Focus on finding the answers to the following questions.

1 How many languages do they speak? When do they speak each of them?
2 What are the differences between their native culture and the culture of the country where they live?
3 Do they think it is important to preserve their native culture and language? If so, how do they do it? If not, why?

4 Share your findings with your classmates. Then discuss the questions.

1 Do the people interviewed share the same views? What do they have in common and in which aspects do they differ?
2 How can you respect the different cultural and linguistic backgrounds of the people you know?

IMAGINE

Imagine a family consisting of one person and his/her pet(s).

1 Read the text and discuss the questions with a classmate.

1 Do you have any pets? Do you consider them part of your family?
2 Do you think a person and his/her pet can be considered a family? Why?
3 How would you describe a family?
4 Can you think of other examples of nontraditional families?

RTV

1 **Match the countries to the characters. Then write their nationalities.**

1 Australia
2 England
3 Japan
4 Scotland
5 the United States

a 

Lisa Simpson is ______.

b 

Merida is ______.

c 

Winnie the Pooh is ______.

d 

Nemo is ______.

e 

Pikachu is ______.

2 **Complete the dialogue using *am*, *is* or *are*.**

Lily: You (1) ______ Ryan, right?
Ryan: That (2) ______ right.
Lily: I (3) ______ Lily and she (4) ______ Emma. She (5) ______ my best friend. We (6) ______ from Colombia and we (7) ______ new here.
Ryan: Hi there! Welcome to the school!
Emma: Thank you! We (8) ______ in the same class.
Ryan: Cool!

3 **Rewrite the sentences from activity 2 using the contracted form of the verb to be.**

1 ______
2 ______
3 ______
4 ______
5 ______
6 ______

4 **Read the dates and complete the sentences.**

1 Taylor Swift (singer) – 12/13/1989
Her birthday is in December.
2 Cristiano Ronaldo (athlete) – 02/05/1985
His birthday is in ______.
3 Chris Hemsworth (actor) – 08/11/1983
His birthday is in ______.
4 J.K. Rowling (writer) – 07/31/1965
Her birthday is in ______.
5 Bruno Mars (singer) – 10/08/1985
His birthday is in ______.

5 **Read the clues and guess the months.**

1 It's after February and before April.
______
2 It starts with J, it has 4 letters and it's not July.
______
3 It's the month before the last month of the year.
______
4 It starts with O and it has 7 letters. ______
5 It starts with A and it has 6 letters. ______

REVIEW 2

1 **Read Damien's text about his family and complete it with the words from the box.**

aunt brothers cousins father
grandma grandpa mother uncle

My name is Damien and I li[illegible]iladelphia, United States, with my parents (my (1) ___________, Jessica, and my (2) ___________, Louis [illegible]d my two (3) ___________, William and Jason. My dad has a sister, my (4) ___________ Michelle, and she has three children, Nicole, James and Alice. They are my (5) ___________. My mother has a brother, my (6) ___________ Tim. He lives with his wife, Rachel, in Chicago. They don't have children, but they have five dogs, so they have a big family. My mother's parents, (7) ___________ Lily and (8) ___________ Joe, live in New York, so we visit them often.

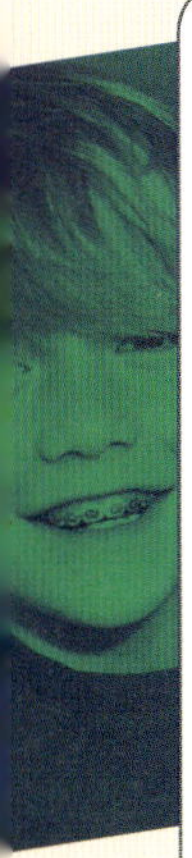

2 **Complete Damien's statements about his family using the verb to be in the affirmative or negative form.**

1 Lily and Joe ___________ my grandparents.

2 William and Jason ___________ my cousins.

3 Rachel ___________ my aunt.

4 Nicole, James and Alice ___________ my siblings.

3 **Write questions for the answers below.**

1 Are you happy today?

Yes, I am.

2 ______________________________

No, they aren't.

3 ______________________________

Yes, we are.

4 ______________________________

Yes, it is.

4 **Match the beginnings and endings of the sentences.**

1 It...	a	☐	isn't my brother.
2 I...	b	☐	isn't windy right now.
3 He...	c	☐	am not at home.
4 They...	d	☐	isn't a sad woman.
5 She...	e	☐	aren't my grandparents.

5 **Look at the images and write sentences using *this*, *that*, *these* or *those*.**

1

____

2

____

3

____

4

____

3

A PLACE TO LEARN

OBJECTIVES

- Talk about your school.
- Identify school facilities, objects and subjects.
- Identify characteristics of a variety of posters and understand their functions.
- Use the structure there to be to talk about existing things.
- Use prepositions of place to say where things are.
- Create a poster.
- Investigate how many students are satisfied with the conditions of the school facilities.
- Reflect on the factors that prevent children and teenagers from attending school and how to deal with this problem.
- Give opinions about a world without schools where children have to be educated at home.

Read the questions and discuss.

1 What does the image represent to you?
2 Where can you learn things?
3 How would you describe your school?
4 Would you like your school to be different? How?

Richmond

#MAKERS DIGITAL

1

2

3

4

5

6

RTV

1 **Look at the images. In which one can you see...**

- a ☐ a teacher with his class?
- b ☐ lots of books?
- c ☐ different kinds of school materials?
- d ☐ sports equipment?
- e ☐ students having lunch?
- f ☐ students conducting experiments?

2 16 **Listen to a podcast and look at the images. Which images show elements mentioned in the podcast? Check the correct answers.**

- a ☐ Image 1
- b ☐ Image 2
- c ☐ Image 3
- d ☐ Image 4
- e ☐ Image 5
- f ☐ Image 6

3 17 **Listen to the podcast again. Then discuss the questions in pairs.**

1. Does your school have all the elements represented in the images? If not, would you like it to have any of them? Which one(s)?
2. Is your school similar to Keith's? In what aspects?
3. In which aspects is your school different from Keith's?
4. Would you like to attend Keith's school? Why?

React!

4 **Write a comment about the podcast.**

KUDOS TO KAY–Episode 216

Discover | Trending | Following | Playlists

WHAT DO YOU THINK OF THIS PODCAST?

Faith Sanders Awesome podcast! Very funny!
February 16, 2018 — Great! Report

Proud Geek I like Math too!
March 25, 2018 — Great! Report

Emma Harris I wish my school was like that. :(
April 1, 2018 — Great! Report

____

POST

I Wonder

5 **Write a question about schools in another country. Then look for the answer.**

____

99 Great! 99 Interact

LANGUAGE 1

1 **Match the school facilities to their definitions. You may use a dictionary to help you.**

1	auditorium	5	laboratory
2	bathroom	6	library
3	cafeteria	7	principal's office
4	gymnasium	8	swimming pool

a [ ] a type of restaurant

b [ ] a room where people do Science experiments

c [ ] a place with special equipment for doing physical exercises

d [ ] a structure filled with water for practicing aquatic sports

e [ ] a room where the school principal works

f [ ] a large room for speeches, lectures and stage performances

g [ ] a place where there is a toilet

h [ ] a room that contains a collection of books

2 **Label the images using the words/expressions from the box.**

correction fluid eraser pen pencil
pencil case whiteboard

1

2
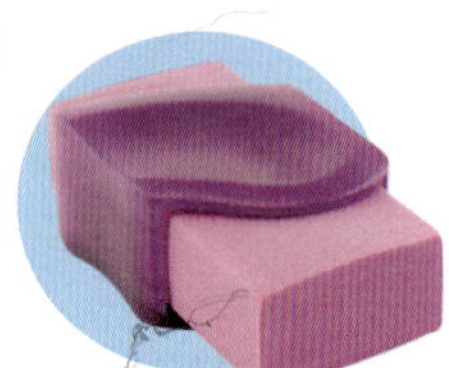

3

4

5

6
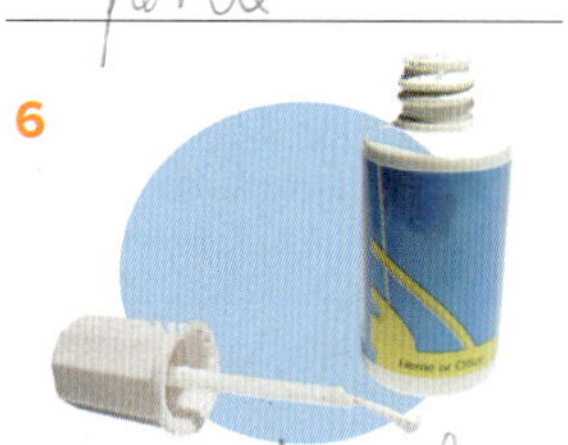

3 **Read the sentences and circle the correct options.**

These are the lockers. Students keep their **books**, **notebooks** and other school stuff here.

1 The words in bold are examples of school **objects** / **uniform**.

2 They are in the **singular** / **plural** form.

Snack Learning

Plural Nouns

pen: pen**s**	watch: watch**es**
library: librar**ies**	paper clip: paper clip**s**

4 **Count and write the plural nouns.**

1

a glue stick
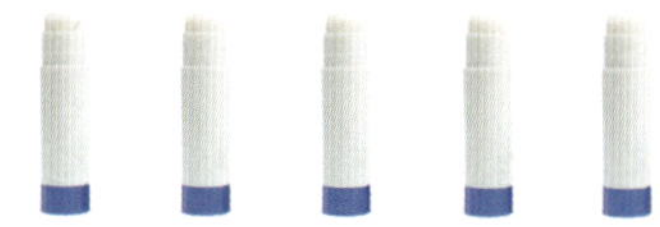
five glue sticks

2

a paintbrush

3
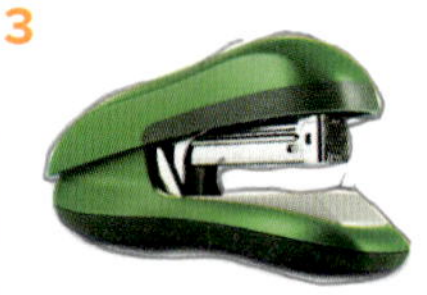
a stapler

4

a dictionary

5
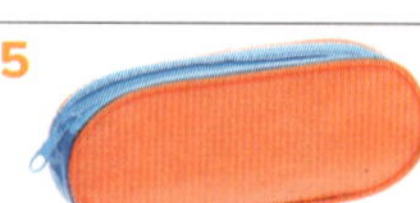
a pencil case

My Glossary

5 **Answer in pairs.**

What objects do you have...

a in your pencil case?

b in your backpack?

c on your desk?

LISTENING AND SPEAKING

1 18 **Listen to Keith giving a tour of his school and identify the places he visits.**

a ____________ d ____________
b ____________ e ____________
c ____________

2 19 **Listen again. Then write T (true) or F (false) and correct the false statements.**

1 ☐ Keith studies at a school named Challenge Middle School.
____
2 ☐ Keith's school has twelve classrooms.
____
3 ☐ There's lasagna for lunch today.
____
4 ☐ Keith's favorite subject is Science.
____
5 ☐ The Math teacher is named Mr. Taylor.
____

Study Space

Buzzwords

"The teachers are ***awesome****."*
What does "awesome" mean in this context? Look it up!

Pronunciation

3 20 **Listen to Keith and notice how he pronounces the words in bold. Does your language have this *th* sound?**

I'm **Keith Mathis** and I live in **South** Houston.
That was Mr. **Smith**, the History teacher.
And these are the **three** new **bathrooms**.
Mr. White is the **Math** teacher.

4 21 **Listen and practice the words below.**

bathroom birthday Math
month three

5 22 **Listen to the sentences in activity 3 again and practice them.**

6 **Plan a short podcast about your school.**

1:15 p.m.

Hello, everyone!
I'm ____________ and I live in ____________. I'm in the 6th grade and I study at ____________. It's a large/small school with ____________ classrooms. It has lots of facilities, like ____________, ____________ and ____________.
Today I'm going to give you a school tour. This is the ____________. This is the ____________. This is the ____________. And this is my classroom. We have ____________ now.
Well, this is my school. I like it because ____________.
See you next time!

7 **Record your podcast and share it on #MAKERS Digital <www.richmondmakers.com>. Use the hashtag #SchoolTour.**

Before Reading

1 **Look at the texts and discuss the questions in pairs.**

1 Which text gets your attention the most? Why?

2 Which similarities and differences can you notice between the texts?

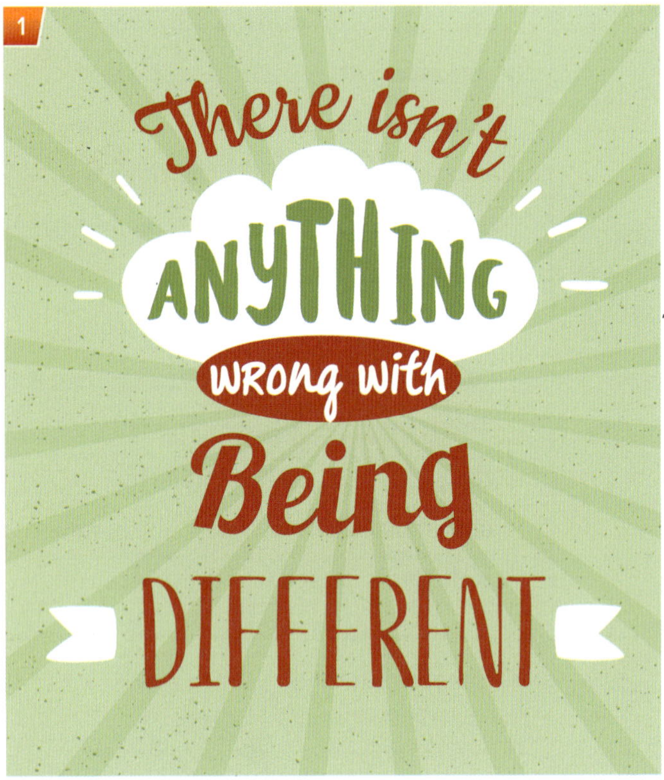

2 Look at the texts and circle the correct option.

1 These texts are...
  a ads.
  b leaflets.
  c posters.

2 We can see them in...
  a restaurants.
  b schools.
  c parks.

3 Check all the correct answers.

1 This kind of text is used to...
  a ☐ give information.
  b ☐ attract people's attention.
  c ☐ tell a fictional story.
  d ☐ persuade people to do something.
  e ☐ irritate other people.
  f ☐ present the author's personal information.

2 What are some characteristics of this kind of text?
  a ☐ It is creative.
  b ☐ It is long.
  c ☐ There is always an image in it.
  d ☐ It is visually attractive.
  e ☐ It is usually colorful.
  f ☐ It doesn't present questions.

While Reading

4 Read the posters in activity 1. Then write which ones correspond to the descriptions below.

a Information poster ______
b Campaign ad ______
c Motivational poster ______

5 Read the posters again and answer.

Which poster...
  a ☐ can be seen in a library?
  b ☐ encourages people to donate books?
  c ☐ asks for suggestions?
  d ☐ suggests that difference is good?
  e ☐ points at something outside it?
  f ☐ doesn't present an order or request?
  g ☐ asks the reader a question?

6 Read poster 2 again and check the signs that convey the same ideas.

1 ☐

2 ☐

3 ☐

4 ☐

5 ☐

7 Complete the sentences about the messages of the posters.

1 According to poster 1, being ______ is positive.
2 Poster 2 asks you to be ______ in that place.
3 According to poster 3, there are people who need your old ______.
4 Poster 4 suggests that your ______ are important.

Study Space

After Reading

8 Analyze the visuals in the posters and discuss.

1 Do they help convey the message of the posters? Why?
2 Which of the visuals appeals to you the most? Why?

9 Are there similar posters in your school? If not, what kind of posters are there?

10 In your opinion, which of these posters is the most effective? Why?

Workbook p. 141

LANGUAGE 2

1 Read the sentences and complete.

1
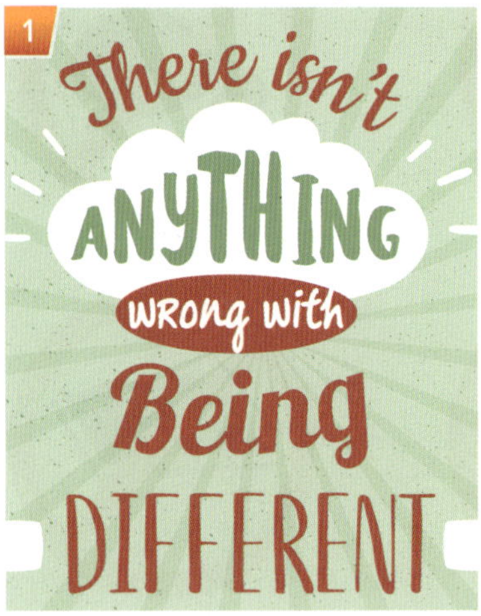

2
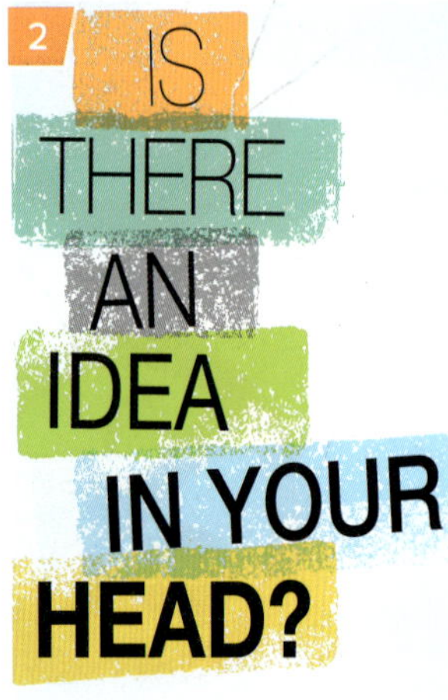

3

a The second part of sentence ______ is in the affirmative form.

b Sentence ______ is in the negative form.

c Sentence ______ is in the interrogative form.

There to Be

Affirmative

There is a library in my school.
There are two swimming pools in my club.

Negative

There isn't a library in my school.
There aren't two swimming pools in my club.

Interrogative

Is there a gym?
Are there books in the box?

Short Answers

Yes, there is. / No, there isn't.
Yes, there are. / No, there aren't.

The structure *there* + verb to be is used to **say that something exists.**

2 Underline the correct form of there to be to complete the sentences.

1 **Are there** / **Is there** many students in your school?
2 **There is** / **There are** two students in the principal's office.
3 **There is** / **There are** a soccer field in the club.
4 **There aren't** / **There isn't** an airport in my town.
5 **Is there** / **Are there** a red pen in your pencil case?
6 **There isn't** / **There aren't** many books in the library.

3 Complete the questions and answer them about yourself.

1 ______ many students in your class?
______
2 ______ anything on your desk?
______
3 ______ an auditorium in your school?
______
4 ______ any books in your backpack?
______
5 ______ many pens in your pencil case?
______

Snack Learning

***A/An* for Singular Nouns**

***a* + consonant sound**
a cafeteria
a backpack

***an* + vowel sound**
an auditorium
an eraser

4 Complete the sentences about your school. Use *a* or *an* where appropriate.

1 In my school there is ______ and there are ______.
2 In my school there isn't ______ and there aren't ______.
3 In my ideal school there is ______ and there are ______.
4 In my ideal school there isn't ______ and there aren't ______.

Study Space

Snack Learning

School Subjects

Art
English
Geography
History
Math
Physical Education
Science

5 Complete the sentences about yourself.

1 My favorite subjects are ____________ and ____________.

2 My least favorite subjects are ____________ and ____________.

3 I am good at ____________.

4 I am not so good at ____________.

Study Space

6 Match the images to the sentences.

1

2

a [ ] Put your books in the box.

b [ ] Leave the books on the table.

Prepositions of Place

7 Look at the images and answer the questions.

1

Where's the mechanic?

____

2

Where are the bikers?

They're behind the bus

3

Where are the colored pencils?

They're in the pencil case

4

Where's the apple?

It's on the book

5

Where's the family?

It's next to the notebook

6

Where's the mechanical pencil?

____

7

Where's the puppy?

____

Workbook p. 141

WRITING

A Poster

Before Writing

1 **Plan your poster.**

1 What is the theme of your poster?

2 What is its purpose?

3 Who is it for?

4 What message do you want to convey?

5 Are there images in it? If so, which one(s)?

Drafting

2 **Write and draw a draft of your poster.**

3 **Share your poster with a classmate and ask for his/her opinion. Make adjustments, if necessary.**

Final Writing

4 **Make the final version of your poster. Publish it on #MAKERS Digital <www.richmondmakers.com> using the hashtag #MyPoster.**

INVESTIGATE

Few   Some   Most of the

__________ students are satisfied with the conditions of the school facilities.

Collect Data

- In small groups, prepare a questionnaire about the conditions of the classrooms and other school facilities. For example, you can ask about the condition of the desks, cleanliness of the walls, temperature and organization of the rooms and quality of the equipment. Don't forget your questions should be clear and objective.
- Decide when you are going to interview the students and how you are going to explain why you are interviewing them.
- Conduct a survey among the students. Choose one of the other classes and interview its students. Remember to write down their answers.

Analyze the Data

- How many students were interviewed?
- How many of them are satisfied with the conditions of the school facilities? How many are not?
- Which is the most praised facility? Why?
- Which is the most criticized facility? Why?

Draw a Conclusion

__________ students are satisfied with the conditions of the school facilities.

1 **Reflect on your conclusion and discuss.**

1 Are you surprised by it? Why?

2 What do the students think about their classroom? What should be done to improve it?

3 What do they think about the other school facilities? What should be done to improve them?

4 What can the students do to improve the conditions of the school facilities?

2 **Share your ideas on #MAKERS Digital <www.richmondmakers.com> using the hashtag #MySchool.**

Makerspace p. 114

LOCAL AND GLOBAL

1 Read the posters and discuss the questions.

1 Who has the right to go to school?
2 Why are you lucky, according to poster 2?
3 What is the contradiction between the two posters?

2 Research and take notes of your findings.

1 How many children and teenagers are not in school in...
 a your country?
 b the whole world?
2 What factors prevent children and teenagers from attending school?
3 Are there any private initiatives, nongovernmental organizations or governmental programs that deal with this problem in your country? What do they do?

3 Do you know any child or teenager who does not go to school? What can you do about it?

IMAGINE

Imagine there are no schools and children have to be educated at home.

1 Read the article. Then discuss the questions with a classmate.

RTV

1 According to the article, is homeschooling an alternative for students all over the world?
2 In your opinion, what are the possible advantages and disadvantages of homeschooling?
3 Would you like to be homeschooled? Why?

4

HOME IS WHERE THE HEART IS

OBJECTIVES

- Identify parts of a house.
- Identify objects and furniture found in homes.
- Use possessive adjectives and the genitive case to identify to whom certain objects belong.
- Write an alternate ending to a comic strip.
- Investigate how many objects students have in their bedrooms.
- Reflect on housing and homelessness.
- Express opinions about open-plan living.

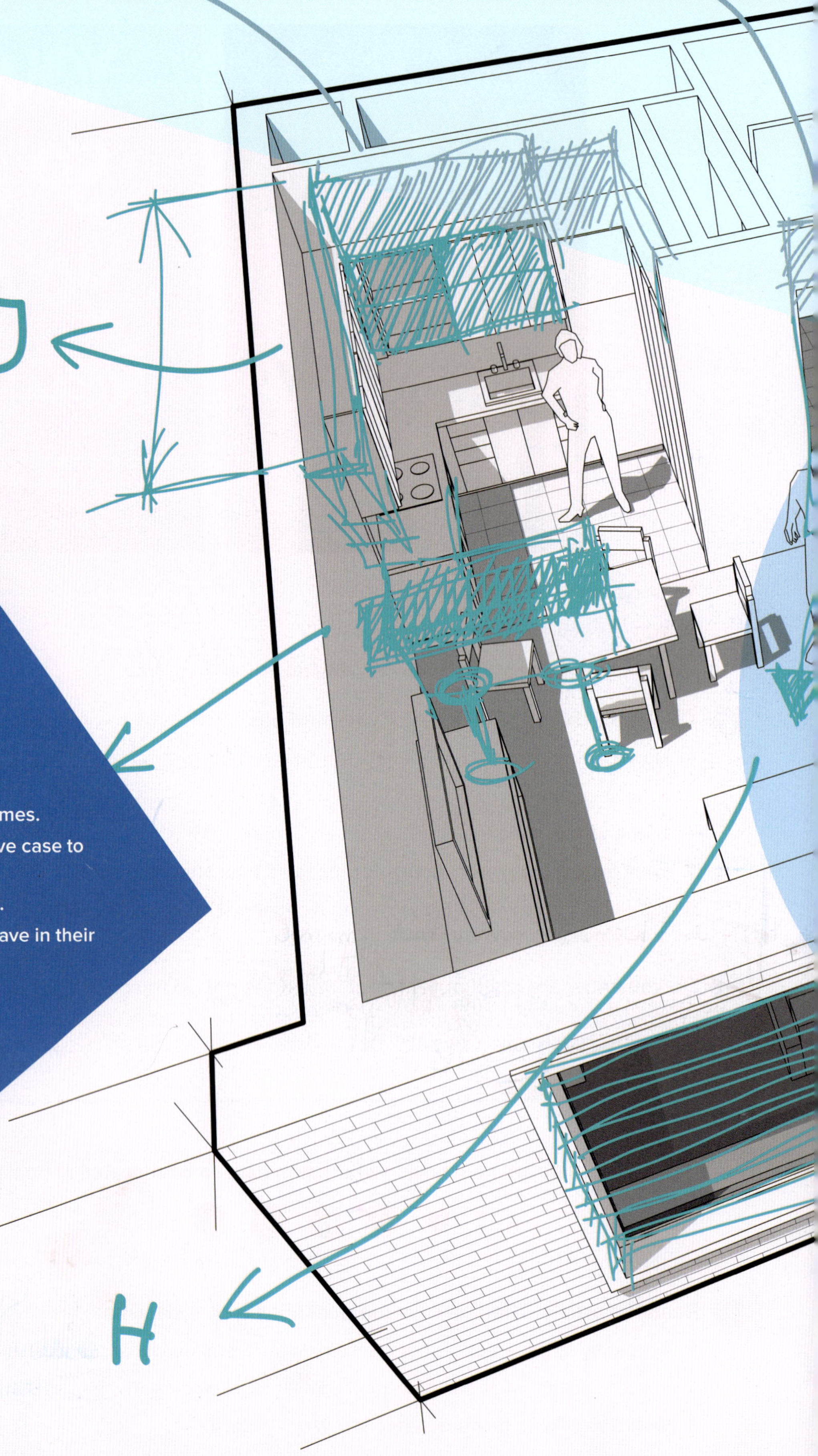

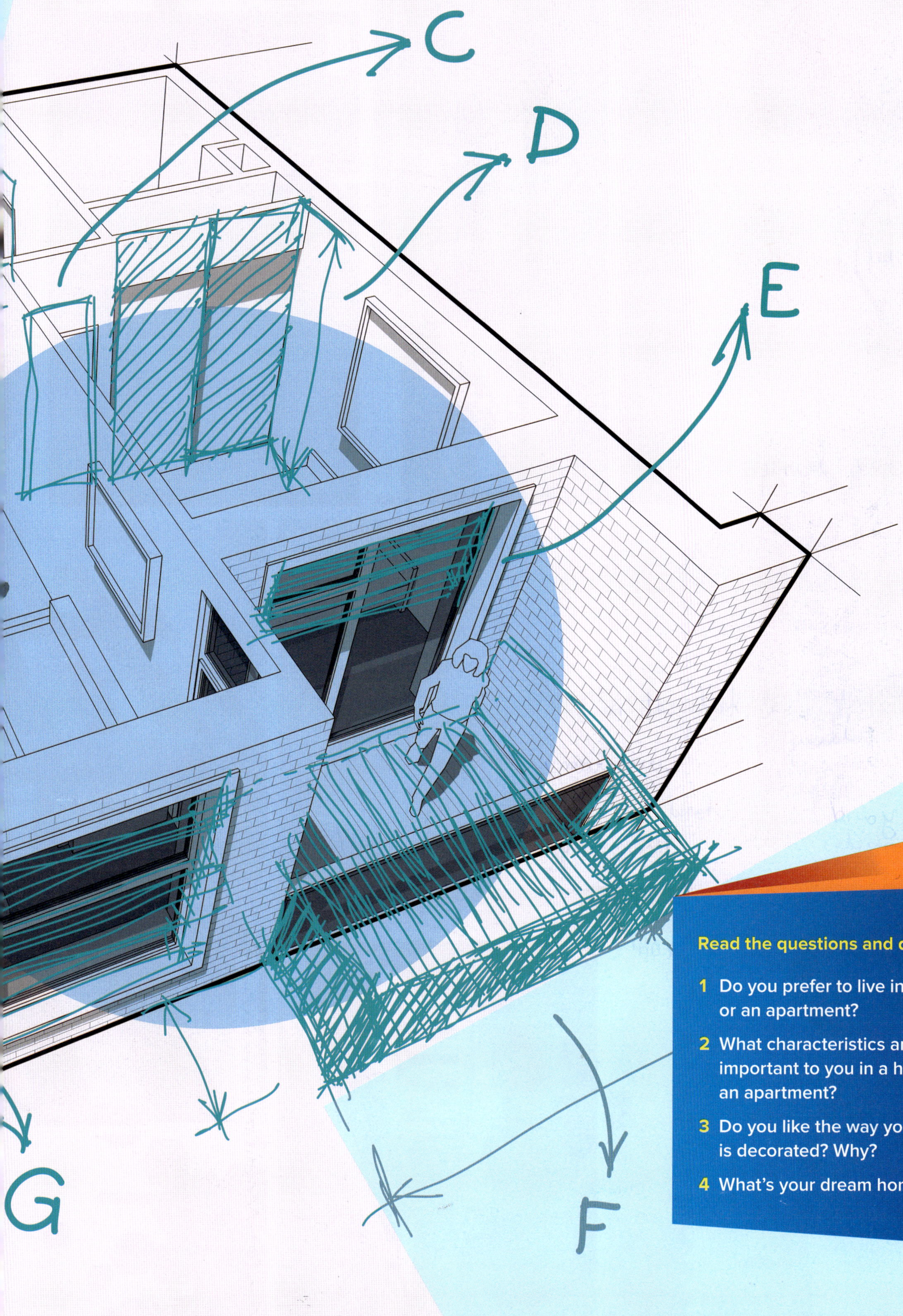

Read the questions and discuss.

1 Do you prefer to live in a house or an apartment?

2 What characteristics are important to you in a house or an apartment?

3 Do you like the way your home is decorated? Why?

4 What's your dream home like?

Richmond

#MAKERS DIGITAL

houseboat

terraced houses

detached house

apartment building

cabin

RTV

1 **Look at the images and discuss the questions in pairs.**

1 What do they have in common?
2 Where do you think these pictures were taken?
3 Which of these types of house are common where you live?
4 Do you know anyone who lives in a house similar to them?

2 **Watch Theo and Bee presenting a house. Why do you think Bee likes it so much?**

3 **Watch the video again. Which part of the house does not appear in it? Circle the correct answer.**

a kitchen
b bathroom
c garage
d bedroom
e garden

4 **Watch the video one more time. Which object is not mentioned in it? Circle the correct answer.**

a bed
b shelves
c sink
d sofa
e window

5 **In your opinion, what are the advantages of living in a house similar to the one in the video?**

6 **Which houses from the images on page 50 could appear in Theo and Bee's vlog? Why?**

React!

7 **Write a comment about the video.**

Makayla Ferreri WOW! That's so incredibly small!
1 week ago — 2 Great! Report

BugRob I love the bedroom! Very cool!
1 week ago — 2 Great! Report

Christine2007 The kitchen is sooooo organized and cute! 😍😍😍
5 days ago — 2 Great! Report

SGCabello_12 I wonder how many people can live in this house.
2 days ago — 2 Great! Report

POST

I Wonder

8 **Write a question about teenagers' bedrooms in other countries. Then look for the answer.**

99 Great! 99 Interact

1 Write the missing letters. Use a dictionary to help you.

2 Use the words from activity 1 to complete the sentences.

1 People usually watch TV in the ______.
2 Some people have big trees in the ______.
3 After dinner, I always clean the ______ table.
4 We have a refrigerator in the ______, next to the sink.
5 There is a bathtub in my ______.

3 Use the words from the box to name the numbered objects in activity 1.

bed chair computer desk dresser lamp mirror nightstand TV wardrobe

1 ______
2 ______
3 ______
4 ______
5 ______
6 ______
7 ______
8 ______
9 ______
10 ______

4 Write sentences comparing your bedroom to the one in activity 1.

In my bedroom there is a chair too. / In my bedroom there isn't a chair.

______

My Glossary

5 Ask and answer the questions with a classmate.

1 What is your favorite room in your home?
2 Are you happy with your bedroom decoration?
3 What objects and furniture are there in your bedroom?
4 Is there a yard in your home? What about a garage?
5 What color is your kitchen?

Study Space

LISTENING AND SPEAKING

1 23 **Listen to Amy's room tour and circle the correct answers.**

1 Amy is making a **video** / **podcast** to talk about her bedroom.

2 She uses boxes to organize the things in her **dressing table** / **closet**.

3 Amy doesn't show her **desk** / **nightstand**.

2 24 **Listen to Amy again and match the objects she has to where they are located.**

1 On her dressing table, she has...

2 On her dresser, she has...

3 On her desk, she has...

a ☐ keys.

b ☐ perfumes.

c ☐ pictures.

d ☐ flowers.

e ☐ a cell phone.

f ☐ a mirror.

3 25 **Listen to Amy one more time and write T (true) or F (false).**

1 ☐ Her pens and her journal are in a drawer.

2 ☐ There are a lot of clothes in her dresser.

3 ☐ Her favorite color is pink.

4 ☐ She collects sunglasses.

5 ☐ There are decorative pillows under the bed.

Buzzwords

*"I can connect my phone to it and **jam out**."*

What does "jam out" mean in this context? Look it up!

Study Space

Pronunciation

4 **Create five compound words using one word from each box.**

bath bed night sun

flower glasses room stand

1 ____________ 2 ____________ 3 ____________ 4 ____________ 5 ____________

5 26 **Listen to the words formed in activity 4 and underline the strongest syllable. Then listen again and practice.**

6 **Plan a tour of your bedroom.**

Hey, guys! Welcome to my bedroom. Let me show you around.
In my bedroom there is/are ____________.
This is/These are my ____________ and this is/these are
my ____________. Here is where I ____________.
This is/These are ____________. That is/Those are ____________.
This is the end of the tour. Let's get out of here!

7 **Record your video and share it on #MAKERS Digital <www.richmondmakers.com>. Use the hashtag #MyBedroomTour.**

READING

Before Reading

1 **Look at the image and answer: what kind of text is this?** It's a comic trip

2 **What are some characteristics of texts such as the one in activity 1? Check the correct column.**

		✔	✖
1	They are usually funny.	✓	
2	There are always images.	✓	
3	The images are always colored.		X
4	They sometimes criticize a situation.	✓	
5	The text is usually in speech bubbles.	✓	
6	They are always divided into three parts.		X
7	There is never a title.		X

3 **Check the correct answers.**

1 Who reads this kind of text?
- a ☐ Only teenagers.
- b ☐ Only adults.
- c ☒ People of all ages.

2 Where do you see this kind of text?
- a ☐ In billboards.
- b ☐ In game websites.
- c ☒ In newspapers (print and online).

4 **Hide the text in the speech bubbles and look at the images. Then discuss the questions with a classmate.**

1 How do you think the two people in the text are related to each other?

2 In your opinion, what are they talking about?

3 How do you think they are feeling? Justify your answer.

5 **Look at the speech bubbles briefly. Which of the items below are mentioned in the text?**

a ☐

b ☒

c ☒

d ☐

While Reading

6 **Read the comic strip in activity 1 and circle the correct options.**

1 Who are the people in the strip?
   a A little girl and her babysitter.
   b A little girl and her mother.

2 Where are they?
   a At the little girl's house.
   b At the older girl's house.

3 In which room are they?
   a In the bedroom.
   b In the living room.

4 What's in the little girl's hand?
   a A remote control.
   b The little girl's cell phone.

7 **Is it correct to say that...**

a the little girl wants to watch TV?

____

b the little girl doesn't know how to turn on the TV?

____

c the babysitter hates SpongeBob?

____

8 **Write B (babysitter) or L (little girl) in the images that represent what their facial expressions convey in the comic strip. Two images will not be used.**

1 happiness

2 anger

3 dislike

4 surprise

9 **Consider the little girl's and the babysitter's feelings in activity 8 and choose the options that explain the reasons for their feelings.**

a ☐ The babysitter thinks the little girl is not behaving properly.

b ☐ The babysitter wants to teach the little girl how to use the remote control.

c ☐ The little girl doesn't get what she wants.

d ☐ The little girl hates SpongeBob.

10 **Analyze the third panel in the comic strip. Then match the questions to the answers.**

1 Why is the word "mean" in italics?

2 Why is the word "hate" in bold and italics?

3 Why does the babysitter use "oooo"?

4 Why is the sentence "I don't like SpongeBob" in small letters?

a ☐ To emphasize it.

b ☐ To express disapproval of what the little girl said.

c ☐ To show that the speaker lowered her voice.

d ☐ To show that the speaker raised her voice.

11 **Read the questions and discuss them with a classmate.**

1 Why do you think the little girl says she doesn't like SpongeBob in the third panel?

2 How does the girl behave in the babysitter's house? Justify your answer.

After Reading

12 **Do you think that, if the little girl had been respectful and polite instead, the babysitter would have let her watch TV? Why?**

13 **What could the little girl have said to the babysitter in order to be more respectful and polite?**

1 Panel 1: ______________________

____

2 Panel 2: ______________________

____

3 Panel 3: ______________________

____

Study Space   Workbook p. 143

LANGUAGE 2

1 Who do the circled words in the comic strip panel refer to? Write B (babysitter) and L (little girl).

1 [ ] He's **my** very favorite.

2 [ ] **My** house, **my** rules.

2 Analyze the panel in activity 1 again and circle the correct options.

The adjective *my* expresses (1) **place** / **possession** and refers to the person who is (2) **listening** / **talking**.

Possessive Adjectives

I	I have two cats and a dog. I love **my** pets.
You	Kate, is that **your** new cell phone?
He	Chocolate is **his** favorite cake.
She	**Her** backpack is on the chair.
It	The channel announced **its** first video.
We	Where are **our** books?
You	Kids, **your** break starts now!
They	Diana and William are late with **their** homework.

Possessive adjectives are used to indicate that something **belongs** to someone.

3 Complete Ellen's text with possessive adjectives.

Hi. (1) ______ name is Ellen and I am 13 years old. This is my house. I live here with mom and dad. They are dentists and (2) ______ office is not far from our house. I also have a brother. (3) ______ name is Phil. He and I go to the same school. We take the school bus every morning. (4) ______ bus is a little old, but it's comfortable. My best friend, Jane, is my classmate and (5) ______ mom is a dentist too!

4 Look at the images and complete the sentences using possessive adjectives.

1

That's my neighbor Mark. And that's Gennaro, ______ cat.

2

That's my sister Janice in ______ car.

3

Those are my friends Clarice and Neil and ______ parents.

4

That's me! Soccer is ______ favorite sport!

5

That's my favorite notebook. ______ cover is red.

6

Those are my classmates and that's ______ Science teacher.

5 Cross out the incorrect possessive adjective.

1 Carol visits **her** / **his** grandfather every Sunday.
2 Bianca and Eveline take **her** / **their** backpacks to school every day.
3 Larry and I buy **her** / **our** jeans at that shop.
4 This is **my** / **your** milkshake. Your milkshake is over there.
5 Sam phones **his** / **their** mother every night.
6 James, why are **your** / **its** shoes dirty?

Study Space

6 Analyze the comic strip sentences and circle the element in the text that expresses possession.

I wanna watch TV. How do you work this?

Y'know, when you're a guest in someone's home, you don't turn on their TV.

Genitive Case

David**'s** dog loves to play.

Cindy**'s** family is very big.

The genitive case ('s) is used to express **possession**.

Snack Learning

Genitive Case with Plural Nouns

These are my **cousins'** medals.
Let's organize the **children's** toys.

7 Write *'s* or *'* to complete the sentences.

1 Our friends ______ cars are in the garage.
2 There are lots of trees in Kelly ______ yard.
3 The children ______ school material is under the bed.
4 My parents ______ bed is new.

8 Look at the images and complete the sentences about possession.

1 Jack

Jack's mirror is in the bathroom.

2 Samantha

______ desk is in the ______.

3 John

______ computer is in the ______.

4 the kids

______ pool is in the ______.

9 Rewrite the sentences using possessive adjectives.

1 Diana's sunglasses are old.
Her sunglasses are old.
2 The giraffe's neck is very long.
______
3 Is that John's cell phone?
______
4 These are my books and Renata's books.
______
5 My parents' bedroom is white.
______

10 Read the clues and write the missing words.

1 My mother's brother = my uncle
2 My aunt's son = my ______
3 My grandma's ______ = my mom and my aunts
4 My ______ parents = my aunt and uncle

Workbook p. 143

WRITING

An Alternate Ending for the Comic Strip

Before Writing

1 Plan the ending.

1 Read the comic strip on page 54 again. Where is the humor in how the strip ends?

2 How could the ending be different?

Drafting

2 Write and draw a draft of a different ending.

3 Share your new ending with a classmate and ask for his/her opinion. Make adjustments, if necessary.

Final Writing

4 Write and draw a final version of your ending. Then photograph and publish it on #MAKERS Digital <www.richmondmakers.com> using the hashtag #AlternateEnding.

INVESTIGATE

all most some few

I frequently use __________ of the things I have in my bedroom.

Collect Data

- Look around your bedroom, open your wardrobe and all your drawers and count all the things you find there.
- Classify everything you have into categories.

Clothes	Shoes	Electronics	Furniture	Other

- Count the total amount of items in each category.
- Categorize everything you have according to the frequency of use.

I frequently use	I sometimes use	I never use

- Count the total amount of items in each category of frequency.

Analyze the Data

- What kind of items do you use more frequently?
- What kind of items do you use less frequently?
- In which frequency category are there more items? Why is that?
- Why do you keep items that you never use?

Draw a Conclusion

I frequently use __________ of the things I have in my bedroom.

1 Reflect on the conclusion and discuss.

1 Why do you have all the things you have?

2 Is there anything you should have more of?

3 Is there anything you should have less of?

2 Share your ideas on #MAKERS Digital <www.richmondmakers.com>. Use the hashtag #ThingsIHave.

LOCAL AND GLOBAL

1 **Analyze the chart below. Then answer the questions.**

Percentage of inhabitants by type of housing (2016)			
	House	Apartment	Other
Croatia	78.9%	21%	0.1%
France	68.4%	31.5%	0.1%
Greece	42.8%	57.1%	0.1%
Ireland	92.5%	7.3%	0.2%
Poland	57.4%	42.5%	0.1%
Romania	63.7%	36.3%	0%

Available at <http://appsso.eurostat.ec.europa.eu/nui/show.do?dataset=ilc_lvho01&lang=en>. Accessed on March 28, 2018.

1 Which country has the highest percentage of people living in houses? ____________________

2 Which country has the highest percentage of people living in apartments? ____________________

3 Which country has the lowest difference between the percentage of people living in houses and apartments?

____

2 **Research and take notes.**

1 What's the percentage of people living in houses in your city/country? What about in apartments?

2 Is there a lot of people living in poor housing conditions in your city/country?

3 Is homelessness a serious problem in your city/country?

3 **Do you know any NGOs or other organizations dedicated to improving housing conditions or helping the homeless find homes? How do they do that? How can you help?**

IMAGINE

Imagine a house or an apartment without walls to divide rooms.

RTV

1 **Read the text. Then discuss the questions with a classmate.**

1 What are the advantages of a home without dividing walls?

2 Were you surprised by the information in the text? Why?

REVIEW 3

1 Cross the odd one out.

1. classroom – lab – bedroom
2. principal – doctor – teacher
3. movie theater – restaurant – cafeteria
4. pen – pencil – whiteboard
5. library – auditorium – notebook
6. notebook – eraser – correction fluid

2 Circle the correct option to complete the sentences.

1 

The cat is **in** / **on** the box.

2 

The green pencil is **between** / **next to** the red and the blue pencils.

3 

Simon is reading **behind** / **under** the blankets.

4 

The dog is **on** / **in front of** the couch.

3 Complete the definitions with the words from the box.

Art Geography History Math Physical Education Science

1. ____________ is the science of numbers and shapes.
2. ____________ is the instruction in sports, exercise and hygiene.
3. ____________ is the study of countries, oceans and mountains.
4. The study of things that happened in the past is called ____________.
5. ____________ studies the physical and natural world.
6. The activity of drawing, painting and making sculptures is called ____________.

4 Look at the images and write sentences.

1 

There are colored pencils in the pencil case.

2 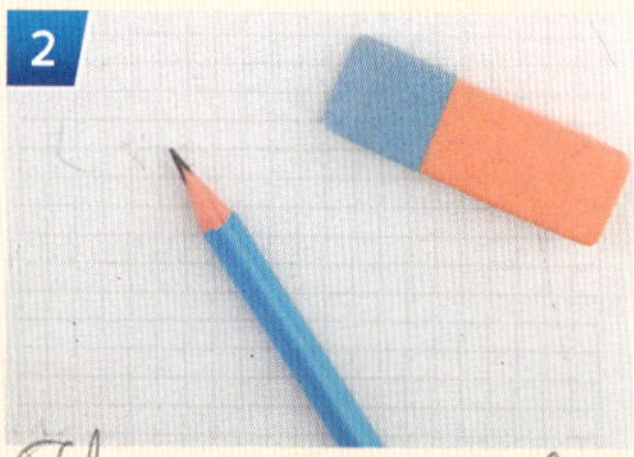

____

3 

____

4 

____

5 Complete the dialogue with the correct form of *there to be*.

Amelia: I'm thinking about changing schools... Where do you study, Oliver?

Oliver: At Riverview. It's a large school!

Amelia: Really? How many classrooms ____________?

Oliver: I think ____________ about 30.

Amelia: It's quite large! ____________ a library?

Oliver: Yes, ____________. A large one with lots of new books!

Amelia: ____________ a good gym?

Oliver: In fact, ____________ two! One in the basement and one on the 3rd floor.

Amelia: Wow! I'll pay a visit to your school.

Oliver: Good idea! I think you should do that!

REVIEW 4

1 **Read the definitions and write the corresponding words.**

1 People use this piece of furniture to read, write or do other work. desk

2 People use this object to check how they look. mirror

3 People turn this on when they need extra light. lamp

4 There are drawers in it, and sometimes a mirror above it. dresser

5 This piece of furniture is usually next to the bed. nightstand

6 People use this piece of furniture to sit on. chair

7 A big piece of furniture where people keep clothes and shoes. wardrobe

2 **Complete the sentences with possessive adjectives.**

1 That's a beautiful bird! Its wings are so colorful!

2 Today is my birthday. I am 12 now.

3 Louisa is sad because her baby is not OK.

4 Rose and I walk our dogs every evening.

5 Helen and Kurt love their new house.

6 Guys, please remove your shoes.

3 **Write sentences using the genitive case and the prompts below.**

1 Paula / husband / in Madrid
Paula's husband is in Madrid.

2 our neighbors / son / a doctor
Our neighbors' son is a doctor

3 Robin / piano / white
Robin's piano is white

4 Peter / restaurant / open now
Peter's restaurant is open now

5 Mandy / shoes / over there
Mandy's shoes are over there

6 Those artists / paintings / very expensive
Those artists' paintings are very expensive

4 27 **Listen to a conversation and match the people from the box to where they are. Two images will not be used.**

Andrew Jen Joey Pacey

1

Andrew's living room

2

Jen's dining room

3

Joey's yard

4

Pacey's bathroom

5

Joey's

6

Jen's kitchen

5 28 **Listen to the conversation again and complete the sentences using the name of the preteens that are talking and the genitive case.**

1 Spaghetti is my favorite food.

2 Max is his dog.

3 That is her English notebook.

4 Her cell phone is on the table.

5

THAT'S WHAT FRIENDS ARE FOR

OBJECTIVES

- Describe people's personalities.
- Say what you and your friends like to do together.
- Identify the characteristics of a chat and understand its purpose.
- Use the present continuous to describe what people are doing at the moment.
- Write messages in a chat.
- Investigate if you spend more time in face-to-face or online interactions with your friends.
- Reflect on the access young people have to the internet in your country and around the world.
- Express your opinion about having a robot as your best friend.

Read the questions and discuss.

1 What comes to mind when you look at this image?
2 In your opinion, do you have many friends?
3 What do you like to do with your friends?
4 What is the best thing about having friends?

Richmond

#MAKERS
DIGITAL

1 Hanging out with my BFFs.

2 Getting together with the best people in the world!

3 Just having fun!

4 Chris is so creative...

5 Time to go to class! And Joey always in the back, trying to hide. He's so shy!

6 About to have a picnic in the park.

7 Sam's helping me study for my tests. He's so intelligent!

RTV

1 Look at the images. What do they have in common? How are they different?

2 In which image(s) can you find the following elements?

		Images
1	People having a good time.	1, 2, 3, 4, 5, 6, 7
2	People studying.	
3	People creating something.	
4	People who are outdoors.	
5	People who are indoors.	
6	People helping each other.	

3 Read the photo captions. What do they have in common? How are they different?

4 Read the caption in image 1 again. What does "BFF" stand for?

a ☐ Big Family Fun

b ☐ Best French Fries

c ☒ Best Friends Forever

5 Would you like to be in any of these images? If so, in which one(s)? If not, why?

6 Discuss the questions with a classmate.

1 Who are your BBFs?

2 Where do you hang out with your friends?

3 How do you and your friends help each other?

4 Do you and your friends take pictures?

5 Do you have any pictures in your bedroom?

React!

7 Write a comment about the images.

I Wonder

8 Write a question about friendship. Then look for the answer.

____

____

____

99 Great! 99 Interact

LANGUAGE 1

1 **Look at the sentences from the photo captions on page 64. Then look at the images again and match the adjectives in bold to their definition.**

1 Chris is so **creative**...

2 He's so **shy**!

3 He's so **intelligent**!

a [ ] A person who feels nervous or embarrassed in the company of other people.

b [ ] A person who is good at learning.

c [ ] A person who has original ideas.

2 **What other words can be used to describe someone's personality? Read and circle.**

3 **Use the words you circled in activity 2 to complete the sentences.**

1 Peter is very ________. He separates his clothes by color in his wardrobe.

2 Kelly's mom says she's ________ because she never helps with the dishes.

3 Dan is so ________! He yells at his classmates all the time.

4 Tiffany is kind and pleasant to everyone she meets. People always say how ________ she is.

5 My cousin is very ________. He loves to meet new people and talk at parties.

6 My neighbors are very ________. They only think about themselves and their interests.

7 I am terrible at telling jokes, people never laugh. I'm not very ________.

My Glossary

4 **Complete the sentences so that they are true about you.**

1 I am ________.

2 My best friend is ________.

3 My classmates are ________.

4 My parents are ________.

5 **Complete the sentences using the verbs from the box.**

get go hang (2x) have (2x) study text

1 I'm about to ________ together with some classmates to work on our Science project.

2 My brothers and I want to ________ a picnic by the river on Saturday. I hope the weather is good!

3 Do you want to meet me after class to ________ for the test?

4 I love to ________ out with my classmates after school.

5 When I'm not at school, I usually ________ my friends to tell them what's new.

6 My sisters and I like to ________ out at the mall in our free time.

7 Let's ________ to the movies! What do you want to watch?

8 My friends and I do lots of things together and we always ________ fun!

6 **Look at the images and complete the sentences using expressions from activity 5.**

1

My best friend and I always have fun!

2

My friends love to ________ at the park.

3

I like to ________ my friends on the weekend so that we can keep in touch.

4

I'm about to ________ with my friends. We want to ________ to watch that new comedy. See you later!

LISTING AND SPEAKING

1 29 **Listen to a dialogue and underline the correct options.**

1 The audio is from a **video** / **podcast**.
2 It's **Josh's** / **Shawn's** birthday.
3 Josh is **at home** / **in front of Shawn's house**.
4 Josh gives Shawn tickets for a **game** / **concert**.

2 30 **Listen to the dialogue again and check the correct options. Sometimes more than one option is correct.**

1 What is Josh and Shawn's favorite sport?

a ☐
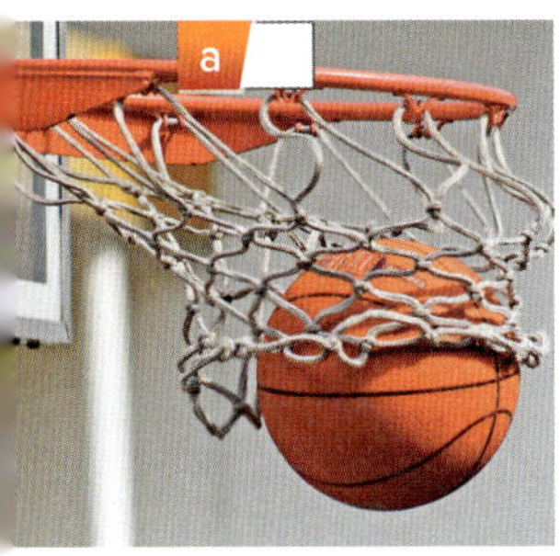
b ☐

c ☐

2 Which activities do Josh and Shawn do together?
- a ☐ Play on the same team.
- b ☐ Play video games.
- c ☐ Go to the beach.
- d ☐ Have classes at school.
- e ☐ Go to the movies.
- f ☐ Watch videos online.
- g ☐ Hang out with their teammates.

3 Which adjectives does Josh use to describe Shawn?
- a ☐ special
- b ☐ sociable
- c ☐ excited
- d ☐ funny

4 Which sentence does Shawn use to invite Josh to enter his house?
- a ☐ "Thanks, man!"
- b ☐ "Come on in."
- c ☐ "Are you for real?"

5 At first, Shawn thinks that the gift is...
- a ☐ a letter.
- b ☐ money.

3 **Read Josh's statement. What does "bang" indicate? Circle the correct option.**

He always meets new people on the bus or on the subway and then, **bang**, he's talking to everyone.

a Something that happens suddenly.
b Somebody that speaks too loudly.
c Something that hurts people.

Buzzwords

*"Are you **for real**?"*
What does "for real" mean in this context? Look it up!

Study Space

4 **Plan a surprise for a friend's birthday.**

Hi, everyone! I'm very excited about today!
It's ______________'s birthday. He/She is
______________. We do a lot of things together!
We like to ______________, ______________
and ______________. Today, I want to surprise
him/her for his/her birthday. I'm about to
______________. Let's go!

5 **Make an audio of your surprise plan and share it on #MAKERS Digital <www.richmondmakers.com>. Use the hashtag #SurprisingMyFriend.**

READING

Before Reading

1 Look at the text. What kind of text is it? Circle the correct option.

a A note.
b A chat.
c A fictional story.

Group: **BFFs**

Anna
Hi, guys! 4:13 p.m.

Mia
Hi! 4:13 p.m.

Charlotte
Hey! I'm studying now. Talk to u later! 4:14 p.m.

Chad
Is your beautiful sister studying with you, Charlie? ❤️ 4:14 p.m.

Charlotte
No, Chad. My beautiful sistert ISN'T studying with me! 😒 4:14 p.m.

Anna
😂 4:14 p.m.

Mickey
Hey, whassup? 4:15 p.m.

Anna
I'm at the mall with dad. We're waiting for Jamie. She's playing air hockey with her friends. 4:15 p.m.

Chad
Why aren't you playing? 4:15 p.m.

Anna
Can you guess? 4:15 p.m.

Chad
Does your foot hurt? 4:16 p.m.

Anna
You don't play air hockey with your feet, silly! 😂 4:16 p.m.

Mickey
Are you eating your favorite brownie? 4:17 p.m.

Anna

4:19 p.m.

Anna
You know me SO well, Mik! LOL! 4:19 p.m.

Mickey
😉 4:20 p.m.

Mia
Yummie! 4:20 p.m.

Chad
Stop that! I'm hungry! 4:21 p.m.

Mickey
Anna, you should have ice cream with your brownie! It's SO hot today! 4:21 p.m.

Anna
Hey, that gives me an idea! Let's have a pool party at my place again! Summer is almost over! 😎 4:22 p.m.

Mia
GR8 idea! I can make my special smoothie! BTW, I'm making some now! 4:22 p.m.

Mia

4:25 p.m.

Chad
Mmm. Love that! 😍 4:25 p.m.

Mickey
And I can take my grandma's cookies! BEST COOKIES EVER! She's baking some now! 4:26 p.m.

Anna
Nice! Let's talk about it tomorrow @ school! 4:27 p.m.

Mickey
Sure! 4:27 p.m.

Chad
Deal! 4:28 p.m.

Mia
Yay! Can't wait! 4:28 p.m.

Charlotte
Pool party? I'm in! 😃 6:02 p.m.

Chad
Can you bring your sister, Charlie? 6:03 p.m.

Charlotte
CHAD!!! 6:03 p.m.

Aa

2 Check the characteristics of this type of text.

a ☐ Formal language.

b ☐ Informal language.

c ☐ Long sentences.

d ☐ Short sentences.

e ☐ Use of visual elements.

f ☐ Use of abbreviations.

3 Who usually writes this type of text? Underline the correct option.

a Only adults.

b Only teenagers.

c People of different ages.

4 Who is the owner of the cell phone? Circle the correct option.

a Anna

b Mia

c Charlotte

d Chad

e Mickey

While Reading

5 Read the text. Then find informal expressions that stand for...

a great. ____________

b you. ____________

c at. ____________

d laughing out loud. ____________

e by the way. ____________

f what's up. ____________

6 Match the questions to the answers.

1 Who is playing air hockey?

2 Who is studying?

3 Who is eating?

4 Who is preparing food?

5 Who is waiting for Jamie?

a ☐ Anna

b ☐ Mickey's grandma

c ☐ Jamie

d ☐ Charlotte

e ☐ Anna and her dad

7 Read the text again and circle the correct option.

Can we say for sure that...

a the group members are best friends? Yes / No

b Chad likes Charlotte's sister? Yes / No

c all the group members have a sister? Yes / No

d Chad wants to eat something? Yes / No

e Chad wants to drink something? Yes / No

f the group members go to the same school? Yes / No

g the group members are all classmates? Yes / No

8 Read the sentences from the text and analyze the use of capital letters. In which sentence(s) does it have the following purposes?

1 No, Chad. My beautiful sister ISN'T studying with me!

2 You know me SO well, Mik!

3 It's SO hot today!

4 BEST COOKIES EVER!

5 CHAD!!!

	Purpose	Sentence(s)
a	Emphasis.	
b	Express excitement.	
c	Express impatience.	

Study Space

After Reading

9 Discuss the questions with a classmate.

1 How do you usually communicate with your friends?

2 Are you part of any message groups? If so, what are they called?

3 What are your favorite expressions in text messages?

4 Do you often use capital letters? If so, with what purpose?

Workbook p. 145

LANGUAGE 2

1 **Look at some sentences from the chat on page 68. Then answer the questions.**

My beautiful sister isn't studying with me!

We're waiting for Jamie.

Are you eating your favorite brownie?

1 Do these sentences refer to the present, to the past or to the future?
To the present.

2 What is the main verb in each sentence?
To study, to wait and To eat

3 Which verb comes before the main verb in all the sentences?
verb to be.

Present Continuous

Affirmative

I **am doing** my homework.
You **are talking** to his mother.
He **is playing** video games.

Negative

It **isn't raining** now.
We **aren't reading** a magazine.

Interrogative

Are they **hanging out** at the mall?
Is she **writing** a text?

Short Answers

Yes, she is.
No, she isn't.

The present continuous is used to talk about **something that is happening at the moment of speaking**.

2 **Return to the text on page 68 and find six more sentences in the present continuous.**

1º: I'm studying now.
2º: Is your beautiful sister studying with you?
3º: She is playing air hockey with her friends.
4º: Why aren't you playing.
5º: BTW, I'm making some now
6º: She's baking some now.

Pronunciation

3 **Are there words ending in *-ing* in your language? If so, how is the *-ing* pronounced?**

4 31 **Listen to some sentences. Then write down the word in each one that ends in *-ing*.**

1 ______ 4 ______
2 ______ 5 ______
3 ______ 6 ______

5 32 **Listen to the sentences in activity 4 again and practice them.**

Snack Learning

Verbs Ending in *-ing*

play: play**ing**
send: send**ing**
make: mak**ing**
sit: sit**ting**

6 **Look at the images. Then write one sentence using each of the verbs given.**

1

read He's reading.
sing He's not singing.

2

write She's not writing
paint She's painting

3

jump They're no jumping
eat She're eating

4

run It's running
sleep It's not sleeping

7 Look at the images in activity 6 again and write a question for each one using the words given. Then give short answers to these questions.

1 book
Is he reading a book?
Yes, he is.

2 movie
Is she watching a movie?
No, she is not.

3 music
Are they listening to music?
No, they are not.

4 fun
Is it having fun?
Yes, it is.

Snack Learning

Let's + Verb

Let's go to the park. **Let's have** a party!

8 Read the statements and invite the speaker(s) to do something.

1 It's my birthday! Let's have a party!
2 It's a sunny day! Let's go to the beach!
3 I'm hungry! Let's eat!
4 We're bored! Let's play!
5 We're tired of studying. Let's have a break!
6 We're late for class. Let's hurry!

Snack Learning

Telling the Time

10:00 a.m.
It's ten a.m. / It's ten o'clock.

10:15 a.m.
It's ten fifteen a.m. / It's a quarter past ten a.m.

10:22 a.m.
It's ten twenty-two a.m.

10:30 p.m.
It's ten thirty p.m. / It's half past ten p.m.

10:37 p.m.
It's ten thirty-seven p.m.

10:45 p.m.
It's ten forty-five p.m. / It's a quarter to eleven p.m.

9 Look at the images and the indications of time. Then write sentences about them.

1

It's eight fifty-four a.m.
She's texting.

2

It's a quarter to ten p.m.
It's sleeping

3

It's seven o'clock a.m.
He's eating

4

It's half past three p.m.
They are watching

Study Space

10 Read the text and complete it using the words from the box.

cooking having let's not helping one thirty p.m. a quarter to ten sitting talking writing

Hey, Fred. How are you doing?
It's (1) one thirty p.m. and I'm at a barbecue at my aunt's house. My whole family is here and everyone is (2) having a great time! Dad is (3) cooking (He loves to do it!) and Mom is (4) talking to her sister. My cousins are (5) not helping, as usual. I am (6) sitting on the porch and I am (7) writing you. The weather is great. (8) Let's go to the park tomorrow and have a picnic! We can meet in the morning, at (9) a quarter to ten, and then I can tell you my plans for the holiday. What do you think?

XOXO
Patricia

Study Space

Workbook p. 145

WRITING

Chat Messages

Before Writing

1 Read the messages.

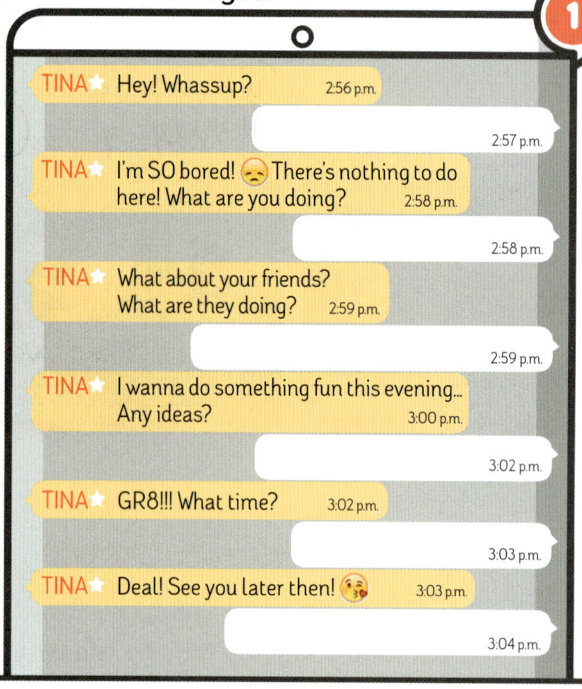

2 Plan your messages to complete the chat in activity 1.

1 What are you doing and what are your friends doing? You can write about what is actually happening or imagine a fictional situation.

2 What would you like to do in the evening? And what time would you like to meet Tina?

3 Are you going to use any visual or informal elements in your messages? If so, which one(s)?

Drafting

3 Make a draft of your chat messages.

4 Share your chat messages with a classmate and ask for his/her opinion. Make adjustments, if necessary.

Final Writing

5 Write the final version of your chat messages. Publish them on #MAKERS Digital <www.richmondmakers.com> using the hashtag #ChatMessages.

INVESTIGATE

less the same amount of more

I spend __________ time interacting with my friends online than face to face.

Collect Data

- For one week, analyze how you interact with your friends.
- Record in a chart who you interact with, if the interaction happens online or face to face and how long each interaction lasts.

Name	Type of Interaction	Duration

Analyze the Data

- How long do you spend interacting face to face with your friends?
- How long do you spend interacting online with your friends?
- Which are usually longer: your online interactions or your face-to-face interactions?

Draw a Conclusion

I spend __________ time interacting with my friends online than face to face.

1 Reflect on the conclusion and discuss.

1 What are the advantages of face-to-face interactions? What about the disadvantages?

2 What are the positive aspects of online interactions? And what are the negative aspects?

3 Which kind of interaction do you feel more comfortable with? Does your preference change according to the situation or to the person you are interacting with?

2 Share your ideas on #MAKERS Digital <www.richmondmakers.com>. Use the hashtag #InteractingWithMyFriends.

LOCAL AND GLOBAL

1 Read the text and discuss the questions.

CHILDREN IN A DIGITAL WORLD

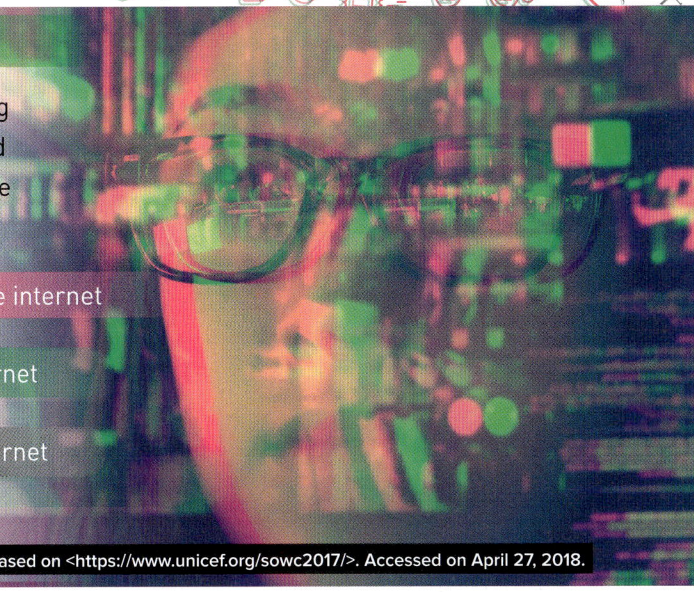

Digital technology can change the lives of disadvantaged young people, offering them new opportunities to learn, socialize and make their voices heard. However, millions of young people are still excluded from the connected world.

346 million young people in the **world** are not connected to the internet

3 out of 5 young people in **Africa** are not connected to the internet

1 out of 25 young people in **Europe** is not connected to the internet

There are **12% more boys** than girls online.

Based on <https://www.unicef.org/sowc2017/>. Accessed on April 27, 2018.

1. Does everyone you know have access to the internet?
2. How does the internet help you in your daily life?
3. How can the internet help disadvantaged people?
4. Why do you think so many young people in Africa are not connected to the internet?
5. Why do you think there are more boys than girls online?

2 Research and take notes of your findings.

1. How many young people are not connected to the internet in...

   a your city? b your country? c your continent?

2. What factors prevent young people from having access to the internet in your country?
3. Is there a large difference between the number of boys and girls connected to the internet in your country?

3 Is the situation in your country similar to any information presented in the text? Which differences do you notice?

4 What can you do to help more young people have access to the internet?

IMAGINE

Imagine having a robot as your best friend.

1 Research into the concept. Bring your research to be discussed in class.

2 Read the article. Then discuss the questions with a classmate.

1. Are robots or any applications of Artificial Intelligence already part of your routine? If so, how?
2. What are possible social, economic and psychological implications of having robots as friends?

RTV

6

AROUND THE NEIGHBORHOOD

OBJECTIVES

- Describe streets and neighborhoods.
- Identify places around town.
- Identify the characteristics and purposes of signs and understand their message.
- Give orders and make requests.
- Write and build a sign for school.
- Investigate the street signs in your neighborhood.
- Reflect on the importance of bilingual signs and their presence in your community and around the world.
- Imagine how a city can be safe without traffic signs.

S/L T/M Q/M Q/J S/V S/S D/D

WIZARDING WORLD

4º tópico: Dê ordens e faça pedidos
5º tópico: Escreva e construa uma placa para a escola
6º tópico: Investigar as placas de rua na sua vizinhança.
7º tópico: Reflita sobre a importância das placas bilíngues e suas presenças na sua comunidade e ao redor do mundo.
8º Imagine como a cidade pode ser segura without sinais de trânsito.

WIZARDING WORLD

S/L T/M Q/M Q/J S/V S/S D/D

Read the questions and discuss.

1. How well do you know your neighborhood?
2. Do you feel like you belong in your neighborhood? Why?
3. Is your neighborhood important to you? How?
4. What's one thing you would like to change in your neighborhood?

Richmond

#MAKERS DIGITAL

Providence, United States

Bogota, Colombia

Bologna, Italy

Tokyo, Japan

RTV

1 **Look at the images. What do they have in common?**

a ☐ They are all located in Europe.

b ☐ They are all capital cities of countries.

c ☒ They all show an area of a neighborhood.

2 **Work with a classmate and discuss the images.**

1 What do you know about those cities and countries? Bogota i perigoro

2 Are there elements in common with the area where you live or study? If so, which one(s)? No, there aren't

3 **Analyze the images and answer: where can you see…**

a stores? In Bologna.

b traffic? In Tokyo

c graffiti? In Bogota

d a small park? In Providence

e the beach? In Cascais

4 33 **Listen to some teens talking about where they live and compare the places they describe with your neighborhood.**

1 Which place is more similar to your neighborhood?

2 Which place is more different from your neighborhood?

5 34 **Listen to the teens again. Based on their descriptions, in which of those neighborhoods would you like to live? Why?**

I would like to live in ______________ because ______________

____

React!

6 **Read the comments below and write a comment about the neighborhood descriptions or about your own neighborhood.**

Chris Dalton #ShareYourNeighborhood I don't really like my neighborhood, there isn't anything interesting about it.

2 days ago — 1 Great! Report

Jamille Brown #ShareYourNeighborhood In my neighborhood there's a Nelson Mandela statue. It's huge!

2 days ago — 1 Great! Report

Cammi2004 I'm from Providence too! My neighborhood is also calm and full of trees. I love it! #ShareYourNeighborhood

7 days ago — ✓ Great! Report

#ShareYourNeighborhood I don't like my neighborhood.

POST

I Wonder

7 **Write a question about a neighborhood from another country. Then look for the answer.**

How is your neighborhood

99 Great! 99 Interact

LANGUAGE 1

1 Read the sentence and guess the meaning of the word "busy". Then look it up in the dictionary and answer.

The streets are very **busy**.

1 How many definitions are there in the dictionary? TWO

2 Which definition is the best for the context of the sentence above? Ocupado

2 Use the dictionary to find out the meaning of the words from the box. Then use these words to describe the streets in the images.

crowded noisy quiet

1

quiet

2

noisy

3

crowded

My Glossary

3 Complete the sentences so that they are true for you.

1 My street is quiet.

2 The street of my school is crowded.

3 My grandparents' street is quiet.

4 Ask and answer the questions with a classmate.

1 Are there stores on your street?

2 Is there a park in your neighborhood?

3 Is there traffic in your neighborhood?

5 What other places are there in your neighborhood? Check.

a [X] bakery

b [ ] bus stop

c [ ] drugstore

d [ ] movie theater

e [ ] museum

Study Space

LISTENING AND SPEAKING

1 35 **Listen again to the teens talking about where they live and match their names to their favorite thing about their neighborhood.**

1 Kimiko
2 Mariella
3 Nicolás
4 Scarlett
5 Vidal

a ☐ It's a very colorful neighborhood.
b ☐ It's very close to the beach.
c ☐ There are many trees in the streets.
d ☐ There are streets for pedestrians only.
e ☐ There is a very good Mexican restaurant.

2 36 **Listen to Mariella's and Vidal's excerpts again and check the correct statements.**

1 ☐ Mariella is living in Milan.
2 ☐ Mariella's neighborhood is usually crowded.
3 ☐ There aren't restaurants in Mariella's neighborhood.
4 ☐ Vidal is from a tourist city.
5 ☐ In the summer, Vidal's neighborhood isn't quiet.
6 ☐ In Cascais, there aren't cool places to hang out.

Buzzwords

*"It's the best place to **chill out**."*
What does "chill out" mean in this context? Look it up!

Study Space

Pronunciation

3 **Are there words ending in *n* in your language? If so, how is the *n* pronounced?**

4 37 **Listen to the sentences and notice how the sounds in bold are pronounced. Is the *n* at the end of words pronounced similarly in your language?**

I'm from Mila**n**. I'm Italia**n**.

Whe**n** I'm **in** Bologna, I like walking **in** the streets. It's a very nice tow**n**.

5 38 **Listen to the sentences and practice them.**

6 **Plan a presentation about your neighborhood.**

Hey, guys! My name's ______________ and I'm from ______________, in ______________. Well, in my neighborhood the streets are ______________.
There are/aren't ______________. There is/isn't ______________.
My favorite thing about my neighborhood is (that) ______________.

7 **Make an audio of your presentation and share it on #MAKERS Digital <www.richmondmakers.com>. Use the hashtag #ShareYourNeighborhood.**

READING

Before Reading

1 Look at the images and answer: what kind of texts are these?

They are signs

2 Check all the correct answers.

1 What are some characteristics of these texts?

- a [x] These texts are short.
- b [ ] They always use two colors.
- c [x] Most of these texts use capital letters.
- d [ ] There is always an image.

2 Who reads these texts?

- a [x] Bikers.
- b [x] Drivers.
- c [x] Pedestrians.
- d [ ] Pilots.

3 What's the purpose of this kind of text?

- a [x] Give instructions.
- b [ ] Describe a place.
- c [x] Provide information.
- d [x] State prohibitions.

4 Where do you see these texts?

- a [x] In the streets.
- b [x] In public places.
- c [x] In parks.
- d [ ] Inside someone's house.

While Reading

3 **Read the signs in activity 1 and answer the questions about who the signs are for, their function and their location.**

1 Which signs...

a are for bikers only? ____________

b are for pedestrians only? ____________

c are for bikers and pedestrians only? ____________

d are for bikers, drivers and pedestrians? ____________

e state a prohibition? ____________

2 Is it correct to say that...

a sign 2 instructs bikers to respect traffic lights? ____________

b sign 5 is located in the middle of a street? ____________

c sign 6 instructs bikers to place their bikes in front of the railings? ____________

4 **Analyze sign 1 and check the correct options.**

1 According to that sign...

a ☐ pedestrians, bikers, drivers and wild animals use the same lane.

b ☐ drivers use one lane; bikers, pedestrians and wild animals use a different lane.

2 Is it probable to see that sign on a street similar to the one below?

a ☐ Yes, it is.

b ☐ No, it isn't.

5 **Where is sign 3 located? Circle all the possible answers.**

a On a crosswalk.

b On a bike lane.

c On a sidewalk.

Study Space

After Reading

6 **In your opinion, are these signs effective? Why?**

Workbook p. 147

LANGUAGE 2

1 **Match the images to the sentences.**

1

2

3

4

a [3] Do not enter.
b [2] Watch for horses.
c [4] Do not disturb.
d [1] Press here.

2 **Read the sentences in activity 1 again and answer.**

1 What is this structure used for?
To give orders or to make requests

2 Which sentences are in the affirmative form?
Sentences b and d

3 Which sentences are in the negative form?
Sentences a and c

Imperative

Affirmative	**Negative**

The imperative is used to give **orders** or make **requests**.

Snack Learning

Contraction

Do not = Don't

3 **Complete the sentences with the verbs in parentheses in the imperative.**

1

don't turn (turn) left.

2

Drive (drive) below 60 km/h.

3

Don't park (park) here.

4

Keep (keep) quiet.

4 In what other situations do people give orders or make requests?

____

____

5 Read the rubrics of the activities in this section and circle the verbs in the imperative.

6 Complete the orders and requests using the imperative of the verbs from the box.

close	open	tell	turn off

1 __________ your cell phone at the movie theater.

2 It's cold here! __________ the window, please.

3 **A:** What's in that box?

B: It's a surprise! __________ it now, wait until the party!

4 **A:** This movie is very good!

B: __________ me the end! I want to watch it!

Study Space

7 Read the imperative sentences in activity 6 again and answer.

1 Which sentence is more polite? Why?

____

2 Is it possible to change the order of the words in that sentence? How?

____

8 39 What are these people saying? Write your guesses. Then listen and check.

1

2

3

4

9 Rewrite the sentences from activity 8 making them more polite.

1 ______________________ 3 ______________________

2 ______________________ 4 ______________________

Workbook p. 147

WRITING

A Sign for School

Before Writing

1 **Plan your sign.**

1. Where is this sign?
2. Who is it for?
3. What is its purpose?
4. Are there images in it?

Drafting

2 **Write and draw a draft of your sign.**

3 **Share your sign with a classmate and ask for his/her opinion. Make adjustments if necessary.**

Final Writing

4 **Write and draw a final version of your sign. Share it on #MAKERS Digital <www.richmondmakers.com>. Use the hashtag #SchoolSign.**

Makerspace p. 115

INVESTIGATE

many few no

There are ____________ street signs for

bikers pedestrians

____________ in my neighborhood.

Collect Data

- Walk around your neighborhood and photograph all the street signs you see.
- Pay attention to all warning signs, regulatory signs and also to guide signs.
- As you photograph them, write down where each one is located.
- Also, take notes about the conditions and visibility of the signs.

Analyze the Data

- How many signs are there?
- What do the signs say? Draw them in your notebook.
- Are the signs in good condition? Are they visible?
- How many of them are for drivers?
- How many are for bikers?
- How many are for pedestrians?

Draw a Conclusion

There are ____________________ street signs for ____________________ in my neighborhood.

1 **Reflect on your conclusion and discuss.**

1. Why are the signs like that in your neighborhood?
2. Is that good or bad? Why?
3. Does your neighborhood need more street signs? If so, which one(s)?

2 **Share your ideas on #MAKERS Digital <www.richmondmakers.com>. Use the hashtag #StreetSigns.**

LOCAL AND GLOBAL

1 **Look at the signs below and discuss the questions with a classmate.**

Singapore

Greece

Japan

Brazil

1 What language is present in all the signs?

2 Why are the signs bilingual?

2 **Research and take notes of your findings.**

What other kinds of bilingual signs are there...

a in your city?

b around the world?

3 **Does your city need more bilingual signs? If so, which one(s)? What can you do about it?**

IMAGINE

Imagine a city without traffic signs.

1 **Research into the concept. Bring your research to be discussed in class.**

2 **Read the text. Then discuss the questions with a classmate.**

1 Is it possible to be safe in a city without traffic signs? How?

2 In your opinion, is the information in the text surprising? Why?

RTV

REVIEW 5

1 **Read people's descriptions of themselves on their social media profiles. Then match each description to an adjective that describes their personality.**

1 You're all so boring! Social media sucks!
2 I really don't want to get out of bed today. Maybe tomorrow.
3 Let's discuss my favorite subject in the world: me!
4 I want to meet new people and keep in touch with my friends.
5 Let's exchange ideas to come up with something completely new.
6 I love to tell jokes and make people laugh!

a [5] creative
b [3] selfish
c [4] sociable
d [6] funny
e [1] rude
f [2] lazy

2 **40** **What time is it? Listen and complete the sentences.**

1 It's 6:42 a.m. I'm having breakfast.
2 I'm waiting for the bus to school. It's 7:45 am.
3 It's 4:30 PM. We're playing video games.
4 They're reading comic books. It's 6:15 PM.
5 It's 7:28 PM. We're having dinner.
6 It's 9:00 PM. They're sleeping.

3 **Number the messages in order.**

a [7] Deal! Meet you there in half an hour.
b [4] Nothing much, just listening to some music and texting my friends. What about you?
c [5] I'm bored.... There's nothing to do! Let's hang out!
d [1] Hey! How are you?
e [2] Great, and you?
f [6] Yeah, sure! Let's go to the park and take a walk or something.
g [8] See ya!
h [3] Same here. What are you doing right now?

4 **41** **Listen to the voice messages. Then underline the correct options to complete the sentences.**

1 Caleb's father **is cooking / isn't cooking**.
2 Caleb's mother **is working / isn't working**.
3 Caleb's sister **is studying / isn't studying**.
4 Caleb **is getting off / isn't getting off** the bus.
5 Caleb **is eating / isn't eating** at the moment.

5 **Correct the statements using the information in parentheses.**

1 I'm eating my favorite brownie. (bake some cookies)
I'm not eating my favorite brownie. I'm baking some cookies.

2 We're hanging out in the park. (study for a test)
We're not hanging out in the park. We're studying for a test

3 Carol is reading her favorite blog. (watch her favorite movie)
Carol isn't reading her favorite blog. She's watching her [illegible] movie

4 I'm texting my friends. (look for information online)
I'm not texting my friends. I'm looking for information online

6 **Write questions using the prompts. Then give short answers that are true about you.**

1 your best friend / watch videos online
Is your best friend watching videos online?
Yes, he/she is. / No, he/she isn't.

2 your mom / work
Is your mom working?
Yes, she is

3 you / listen to music
Are you listening to music?
No, I am not

4 your dad / ride a bike
Is your dad riding a bike?
No, he isn't

5 your teachers / take a break
Are your teachers talking a break?
No, they aren't

REVIEW 6

1 Analyze the signs and match them to their probable location.

1

2

3

4

a [3] restaurant
b [2] bus stop
c [4] museum
d [1] park

2 Frequently, there isn't any punctuation in signs. Rewrite the text from signs 1 and 3 from activity 1 using the correct punctuation.

1: Caution! don't touch dinosaurs!
3: Come in we're open!

3 Read the sentences and write the name of the corresponding location.

1 Buy two and get one free.
store

2 Do not touch the artwork.
Work

3 Pick up after your dog.
Park

4 Give me two croissants, please.
Bakery

5 Don't talk during the film.
Movie theater

6 Take the 52 to the city center.
Bus top

4 Complete the sentences about the signs.

1

a The limit is below 50 km/h.
b The limit is not above 50 km/h.

2

a Don't park here after 8 p.m.
b Park here between 8:30 a.m. and 8 p.m.

5 Complete the dialogues using the verbs from the box in the affirmative or negative form.

come in   forget   open   tell

1 **Mark:** Hello.
Peter: Hey, Mark. Tell me your address, please.
Mark: It's 25 Cloud Street. Where are you?
Peter: I'm at the store.
Mark: Oh, great! Don't forget the chips and the water.
Peter: OK.
Mark: See you soon!
Peter: Bye!

2 *Ding-dong*
Mark: Come in! The door is open.
Peter: Hi, Mark. Happy birthday! Here.
Mark: A present? Oh, thank you so much!
Peter: You're welcome. Open it!
Mark: A Star Wars T-shirt! It's great, I love it!

7

SO MUCH FUN!

OBJECTIVES

- Talk about free-time activities and hobbies.
- Identify leisure activities, musical instruments and periods of the day.
- Identify the characteristics of a blog post and understand its purpose.
- Use the simple present to talk about something that is true in the present or activities that are part of one's routine.
- Describe how frequent some activities are in one's routine.
- Ask questions about things and activities, frequency and the time when something happens.
- Write a blog post.
- Investigate whether you spend most of your free time doing group or individual activities.
- Reflect on the extent to which the culture of your country has been influenced by that of English-speaking countries.
- Give opinions about a world in which people have nothing to do in their free time.

Read the questions and discuss.

1. What comes to mind when you look at this image?
2. What do you like to do in your free time?
3. Do you think you have enough free time? Why?
4. Are there any hobbies you would like to try? If so, which one(s)?

Richmond

#MAKERS DIGITAL

Answer the questions and find out!

1. Who would you like to be friends with?

2. How would you describe yourself?
   A Active and energetic.
   B Tech-savvy and curious.
   C Creative and imaginative.
   D Practical and generous.

3. What do you do to relax?
   A I exercise.
   B I play video games.
   C I read books.
   D I play with my pet.

4. What school subject are you best at?
   A Physical Education.
   B Computer Science.
   C Art.
   D Geography.

5. It's Saturday, a perfect day to…
   A ride my bike in the park.
   B watch a tech tutorial online.
   C go to the movies.
   D raise money for charity.

6. Which kind of TV show do you prefer?
   A Sports shows.
   B Sci-fi movies.
   C Music shows.
   D Documentaries.

7. Which school club would you like to join?
   A Adventure Club.
   B Robotics Club.
   C Book Club.
   D Save Endangered Species Club.

Score: Count the number of A, B, C and D answers and write it down.

A ______ B ______ C ______ D ______

Results

More As – You got: Sports
You should practice sports! It's a great way to exercise and there are plenty of options. You can participate in team sports, such as soccer and basketball, or do individual activities, such as running and swimming. You can also have dance lessons!

More Bs – You got: Technology
You enjoy technology! It's great fun and there are many options for this hobby. You can create and maintain a blog or a vlog and play computer games. You can even build robots and write programs to get them working!

More Cs – You got: Art
You have fun with art! You can read books, listen to music or watch movies. You can also express yourself artistically through drawing, writing, acting, singing, dancing or playing a musical instrument. You can even make jewelry or cook.

More Ds – You got: Social Causes
You have a generous spirit, so you should do volunteer work! You can be a volunteer in animal shelters, summer camps, libraries and museums. You can also help charities by promoting fundraising events or collecting clothes or food for donation. Make a difference in your community!

LISTENING AND SPEAKING

1 42 **Listen to a pollster interviewing a girl and a boy. Then complete the forms according to what they say.**

Research: Free-time Activities

Interview 1 | Name: ____ Age: ____

Free-time Activities

go online	☐	play sports	☐
go to the movies	☐	read books	☐
listen to music	☐	watch TV	☐
hang out with friends	☐	play video games	☐

other activities ____

Hobby ____

Interview 2 | Name: ____ Age: ____

Free-time Activities

go online	☐	play sports	☐
go to the movies	☐	read books	☐
listen to music	☐	watch TV	☐
hang out with friends	☐	play video games	☐

other activities ____

Hobby ____

2 43 **Listen again to the pollster interviewing Charlie and Gabriel. Then write C (Charlie) or G (Gabriel).**

1 ☐ I listen to music online.

2 ☐ I like to participate in competitions.

3 ☐ I love music.

4 ☐ I love to watch *Andi Mack*.

5 ☐ The interviewer and I have the same hobby.

Study Space

Pronunciation

3 44 **Listen to Charlie and notice how she pronounces the sounds in bold. Are they all pronounced in the same way?**

I'm **Ch**arlie.

Not mu**ch**.

I wa**tch** **T**V a bi**t**.

4 45 **Listen to pairs of words. Then check the word in each pair that has the same sound as the final sound in "not".**

	1st word	2nd word
1		
2		
3		
4		
5		

5 **Practice the pairs of words below.**

1 chalk / talk

2 beach / beat

3 arch / art

4 what / watch

5 cat / catch

6 **Think about your free-time activities. Interview a classmate then answer his/her questions.**

Pollster: Excuse me. Can I ask you a couple of questions about free-time activities?
Interviewee: Sure.
Pollster: Your name, please?
Interviewee: ______________
Pollster: Age?
Interviewee: ______________
Pollster: What do you usually do in your free time?
Interviewee: I usually ______________ and ______________. I sometimes ______________ too.
Pollster: And do you have any hobbies?
Interviewee: ______________
Pollster: Thanks for answering my questions!
Interviewee: No problem!

7 **Record an audio of your interview and share it on #MAKERS Digital <www.richmondmakers.com>. Use the hashtag #FreeTimeInterview.**

READING

Before Reading

1 Look at the text and underline the correct options.

1 We can find this kind of text **on the internet** / **in a magazine**.

2 This text is **an e-mail** / **a blog post**.

www.richmond.com.br

THE ADVENTURES OF A 21st-Century Girl

HOME | ABOUT ME | CONTACT

January 13, 2019 | 6 comments

Hey, everybody!

As you all know, I like to do all sorts of things in my free time. I always play sports because I enjoy being active. My favorite sports are soccer, baseball and tennis. I don't play tennis very well and I don't often win a match, but who cares? It's lots of fun! Oh, and I usually jump on my trampoline too!

I'm also creative and I love to draw and write stories and poems about my drawings (I usually post them here!). I also read loads of dystopian books, listen to hip-hop and watch movies and series. So, as you can see, I do lots of things in my free time.

The news today is that I have a new hobby! I'm into photography now! I take my camera everywhere and take pictures nonstop. I love it! Photography is a great hobby and it doesn't have to be expensive (you can even use your smartphone camera!), so anyone can do it!

If you want to see some of my pictures, click here.

What about you? What do you do in your free time? Do you have any hobbies?

Rachel

Search this blog

SEARCH

Blog Archive

2019
2018
2017
2016

Gallery

Recent Posts

Free Time and Hobbies
Happy New Year
My Favorite Things
Friends Are Forever
I Love Art

2 Look at the text again. Then write T (true) or F (false).

1 Why do people write this kind of text?

a [ ] To impartially inform readers of daily news around the world.

b [ ] To express their ideas, thoughts and feelings about topics of their interest.

c [ ] To share knowledge on things they know a lot about.

2 What are the characteristics of this kind of text?

a [ ] It doesn't contain a title.

b [ ] It is usually informal.

c [ ] No punctuation is used.

d [ ] The text has a beginning, a middle and an end.

e [ ] The paragraphs are usually short.

f [ ] It can contain links, images and videos.

g [ ] Readers can't comment on it.

While Reading

3 Read the text and answer the questions.

1 What is the blog called?

____

2 Who is the author of the post?

____

3 When did she start her blog?

In ______________________________.

4 What is the post called?

____

5 When was it published?

On ______________________________.

6 How many people commented on the post?

____

4 Read the post again and check the categories that best describe its content.

a [ ] school

b [ ] family

c [ ] free time

d [ ] friends

e [ ] hobby

f [ ] photography

5 Look at the images and check the one that represents something that Rachel does not do in her free time.

a [ ]

b [ ]

c [ ]

d [ ]

e [ ]

f [ ]

6 Read the post again and check the statements that are true about it. Then cross out the false information in the other statements and correct it.

1 [ ] Rachel isn't an active girl. ____________

2 [ ] She has two favorite sports. ____________

3 [ ] She thinks playing tennis is fun. ____________

4 [ ] She has a trampoline. ____________

5 [ ] She likes reading romantic books. ____________

6 [ ] She likes listening to hip-hop. ____________

Buzzwords

*"I'm **into** photography now!"*
What does "be into" mean in this context? Look it up!

Study Space

After Reading

7 Would you like to follow Rachel's blog? Why?

8 Do you have a blog? If so, what is it about? If not, would you like to have one? What would you write about?

Workbook p. 149

LANGUAGE 2

1 **Read the sentences and answer the questions.**

1 Do you have any hobbies?
2 I don't play tennis very well.
3 I also read loads of dystopian books, listen to hip-hop and watch movies and series.

a Do the sentences refer to the present or to the past? Present
b Which sentence is in the affirmative form? 3
c Which one is in the negative form? 2
d Which one is in the interrogative form? 1

Simple Present

Affirmative

I **have** a new hobby.
You **play** baseball well.

Negative

We **don't jump** on the trampoline.
They **don't read** dystopian books.

Interrogative

How often do you **watch** TV?
What do you **do** in the evening?
When do you **go** to the movies?
Do you **like** photography?

Short Answers

Yes, I do.
No, I don't.

The simple present is used to talk about **something that is true in the present or activities that are part of a person's routine.**

2 **Write questions using the prompts. Then answer them about yourself.**

1 you / have / brothers and sisters
Do you have brothers and sisters? No, I don't

2 your parents / read / lots of books
Do you parents read lots of book? Yes, they do.

3 you and your friends / hang out / every day
Do you and your friends hang out every day? No, I don't

Snack Learning

Expressions of Frequency

every day
once a day/week/month/year
twice a day/week/month/year
three times a day/week/month/year

3 **Match the parts of the sentences. Then write full sentences using the verbs in parentheses in the affirmative or negative forms so that they are true for you.**

1 I (go)...
2 My parents (speak)...
3 I (read)...
4 In my house, we (watch)...
5 I (ride)...
6 My friends and I (hang out)...

a [3] comic books once a week.
b [4] sports on TV twice a week.
c [1] to the movies twice a month.
d [5] my bike to school every day.
e [2] English fluently.
f [6] every day after class.

1 I go/don't go to the movies twice a month.
2 My parents don't speak English fluently
3 I don't read comic books once a week
4 In my house, we watch sports on TV twice a week
5 I don't ride my bike to school every day
6 My friends and I don't hang out every day after class.

4 **Answer the questions about yourself.**

1 How often do you go to the movies?
Three time a year

2 How often do your friends go to your place?
Once a year

3 How often do you check your social media feeds?
I check my social media every day

4 How often do your parents text you?
Twice a week

5 How often do you go to the school library?
Four time at month

5 Circle the correct question word to complete each sentence. Then discuss these questions with a partner.

1 **What** / **How often** sports do you play?
2 **What** / **When** do you have classes at school?
3 **How often** / **What** do you take selfies?
4 **When** / **What** do you usually do in the afternoon?
5 **How often** / **When** are summer vacations in your country?

6 Complete the conversation between Mason and Grace with the affirmative, negative or interrogative forms of the verbs in parentheses. Use the simple present.

Mason: Hello, Grace!
Grace: Hi, Mason!
Mason: (1) ______ you ______ (study) here?
Grace: Yes, I do. I (2) ______ (have) drawing lessons twice a week.
Mason: Great! What (3) ______ you ______ (think) of the course?
Grace: I (4) ______ (love) it! (5) ______ you ______ (study) here too?
Mason: No, I don't. I (6) ______ (teach) here.
Grace: Really? What (7) ______ you ______ (teach)?
Mason: I (8) ______ (teach) blog design to kids and teenagers.
Grace: Cool! I (9) ______ (know) much about blog design.
Mason: So you should take a course with me!
Grace: Good idea! I'll talk to my parents about that.

Adverbs of Frequency

100%	I **always** play sports.
	I **usually** play the guitar.
	They **often** play video games.
	I **sometimes** take a good picture.
0%	We **never** win a tennis match.

Adverbs of frequency are used to say **how frequently we do things or how frequently they happen.**

Snack Learning

Position of Adverbs of Frequency

Adverbs of frequency usually go before the verb (I **always go** to school with my sister.), but they go after the verb to be (I **am always** busy.).

7 Ask and answer in pairs.

cook	have picnics
go for a walk	ride your bike
go to the movies	study for tests
hang out with your friends	text your friends

A: How often do you ______ on the weekend?
B: I always/usually/often/sometimes/never ______ on the weekend.

8 Rewrite the sentences adding an adverb of frequency so that they are true for you.

1 I watch TV in bed.
______
2 My friends and I go to parties together.
______
3 I am tired in the evening.
______
4 My classmates go to school by bus.
______
5 I am sleepy in the morning.
______

9 Complete the questions. Then ask them to a classmate and answer his/her questions.

1 What do you do ______?
2 When do you ______?
3 How often do you ______?

Study Space   Workbook p. 149

WRITING

A Blog Post

Before Writing

1 **Plan your blog post.**

1. What is your blog about? Does it focus on a specific topic? If so, which one?
2. Who are your readers? What are their interests?
3. What are you going to write about in this post? Are your readers interested in this topic?
4. How are you going to organize the ideas in your post? What are you going to talk about at the beginning, in the middle and at the end of your text?
5. What is the title of your post?
6. Do you want to include an image, a video or a link in your post? If so, what is it about?

Drafting

2 **Write a draft of your blog post.**

TRAVELLING AROUND THE EUROPE

Travelling is my passion since I was a little girl. Every end of the year I travel with my family to the Europe. We love to visit museum, castles, restaurants and other nice places.
What about you? What do you do when you travel?

3 **Share your blog post with a classmate and ask for his/her opinion. Make adjustments, if necessary.**

Final Writing

4 **Make the final version of your blog post. Publish it on #MAKERS Digital <www.richmondmakers.com> using the hashtag #MyBlogPost.**

INVESTIGATE

group individual

I spend most of my free time doing individual activities.

Collect Data

- For a week, record all the activities you do in your free time and how long you spend doing each of them.

Activity	Time Spent Doing It
Studying Italian	Fourteen hours
Watching tv	Eight hours
Doing my homework	Fifteen hours

Analyze the Data

- Analyze the activities in your list to decide if they are individual or group activities. Some may be difficult to classify. For example, if you play video games alone in your house but play with other people online, is it an individual or a group activity?
- Write down the amount of time you spend doing each of the activities during a week.
- Add up the amount of time you spend on individual free-time activities and on group ones during a week.

Draw a Conclusion

I spend most of my free time doing individual activities.

1 **Reflect on the conclusion and discuss.**

1. In your opinion, what are the advantages of spending some of your free time on your own and some of it in the company of other people?
2. Are there activities that you usually do on your own that you could do with a group or vice versa? How would the dynamics of this activity change?

2 **Share your ideas on #MAKERS Digital <www.richmondmakers.com>. Use the hashtag #FreeTimeActivities.**

Makerspace p. 116

LOCAL AND GLOBAL

1 Look at the images and answer the questions.

1 Which of these items are you familiar with? Check them.

2 Which of them are originally from English-speaking countries?

2 Research and take notes of your findings.

1 Are the items in activity 1 famous in your country?

2 What are the most popular TV programs in your country? How many of them were originally produced or filmed in English-speaking countries? And how many of them were produced or filmed in your country?

3 What are the most popular songs in your country? How many of them are in English? How many are in your language?

4 What are the movies being played in the theaters in your country? How many of them are American productions or are in English? How many of them were filmed or produced in your country?

5 What are the most popular sports in your country? Are any of them typically associated with an English-speaking country?

3 Share your findings with your classmates. Then discuss the questions.

1 How present are foreign cultural elements in your country?

2 Has your country's culture been influenced by English-speaking countries? If so, how?

IMAGINE

Imagine a world in which people have nothing to do in their free time.

1 Research about the concept. Bring your research to be discussed in class.

RTV

2 Read the blog post. Then discuss the questions with a classmate.

1 According to the post, is it important to do nothing sometimes? Why?

2 In your opinion, is the information in the post surprising? Why?

8

EVERYDAY LIFE

OBJECTIVES

- Describe a person's routine.
- Identify the characteristics of a weekly schedule and understand its purpose.
- Infer information from a weekly schedule.
- Describe the means of transportation used to get somewhere.
- Write a weekly schedule.
- Investigate how much free time students have.
- Reflect on the usefulness of bilingual content on the internet.
- Reflect on the possibility of schools not having fixed schedules.

Read the questions and discuss.

1 Do you like having a routine? Why?

2 What do you do every day?

3 In your opinion, do your classmates have a similar routine?

4 Do you know anyone who has a routine completely different from yours?

Richmond

#MAKERS
DIGITAL

1

2

3

4

5

RTV

1 **Look at the images and discuss the questions in pairs.**

1 Which image could be used to represent your routine?

2 Would you like to do any of the activities represented in the images? If so, which one(s)? If not, why?

2 **In your opinion, do you have a usual or an unusual routine? Why?**

3 **Watch the video about Lucy's routine. Which image best represents it?**

4 **What does Lucy do? Check the correct answer.**

a ☐ She takes photographs of trees.

b ☐ She takes photographs of sloths.

c ☐ She saves sloths.

d ☐ She saves endangered species.

5 **Watch the video again and use the words from the box to complete the sentences.**

calendar difficult great relax sleep year

1 Lucy has a __________ job.

2 She travels to Costa Rica every __________.

3 She takes photographs for a __________.

4 Sloths are __________ to find.

5 Sloths __________ a lot.

6 The calendar reminds us to __________ like a sloth.

6 **Would you like to have a routine like Lucy's? Why?**

React!

7 **Write a comment about the video.**

BM Twins Great video! Loved learning more about the routine of a wildlife photographer!

1 week ago 11 Great! Report

Tyler Moore My routine is totally different from Lucy's! I take a shower, then I go to school. When I come home, I have lunch and study. Then I watch some videos online, have dinner and go to sleep.

3 weeks ago 6 Great! Report

JenniferMathews When I grow up, I want to have a routine like Lucy's: travel to different places, be in contact with nature and photograph animals. Giant thumbs up!

2 months ago 1 Great! Report

____

____

POST

I Wonder

8 **Write a question about the daily routine of students from another country. Then look for the answer.**

____

____

99 Great! 99 Interact

LANGUAGE 1

1 Match the actions to the images.

brush my teeth	go to school
do my homework	read a book
get dressed	ride a bike
get home	take a shower
get up	watch TV
go to bed	

1

2
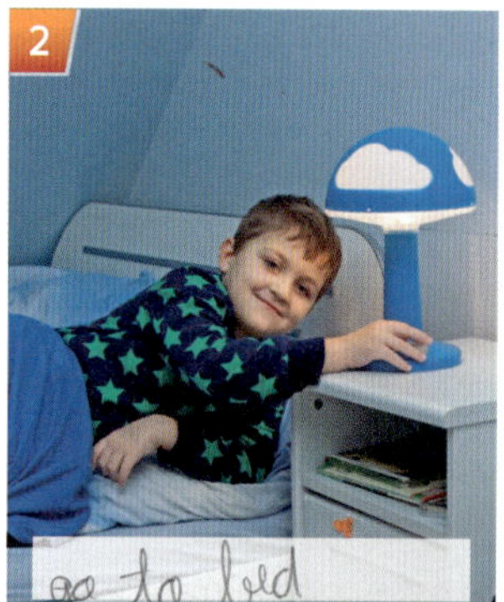

3

4

5

6
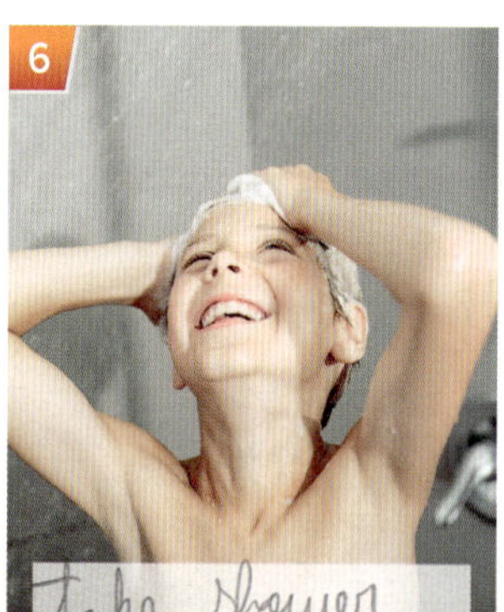

7

8

2 Use the expressions from activity 1 to complete the timeline below according to your routine.

MORNING

AFTERNOON

EVENING

3 At what time of the day do you have the meals below? Add them to the timeline in activity 2.

have breakfast

have lunch

have dinner

My Glossary

4 Complete the sentences about your routine.

1 In the morning, I ____________.

2 Before school, I ____________.

3 After school, I ____________.

4 After dinner, I ____________.

5 In the afternoon, I ____________.

6 In the evening, I ____________.

LISTENING AND SPEAKING

1 46 **Listen to Gabby's routine and check the correct statements.**

1 ☐ Gabby wakes up very late.
2 ☐ Gabby goes to school in the morning.
3 ☐ Gabby gets dressed for school after breakfast.
4 ☐ Gabby takes a shower in the morning.
5 ☐ Gabby does her homework before dinner.

2 47 **Listen to Gabby again and rewrite the sentences to make them true about her.**

1 I get up at 7:30 a.m.

____

2 I take some time to make my breakfast.

____

3 After I brush my teeth, I take a shower.

____

4 After lunch, I take a shower.

____

5 After my shower, I do my homework.

____

3 **Read Gabby's sentences and check their correct meaning.**

1 "My alarm goes off."
- a ☐ My alarm stops.
- b ☐ My alarm begins to sound.
- c ☐ My alarm is set.
- d ☐ My alarm breaks.

2 "I'm all set."
- a ☐ I look good.
- b ☐ I'm ready.
- c ☐ I'm fast.
- d ☐ I'm tired.

3 "I pick out a fresh pair of pajamas."
- a ☐ I get my favorite pair of pajamas.
- b ☐ I reuse a pair of pajamas.
- c ☐ I choose a clean pair of pajamas.
- d ☐ I buy a new pair of pajamas.

4 **In pairs, ask and answer the questions below. Then use your own ideas to make new questions.**

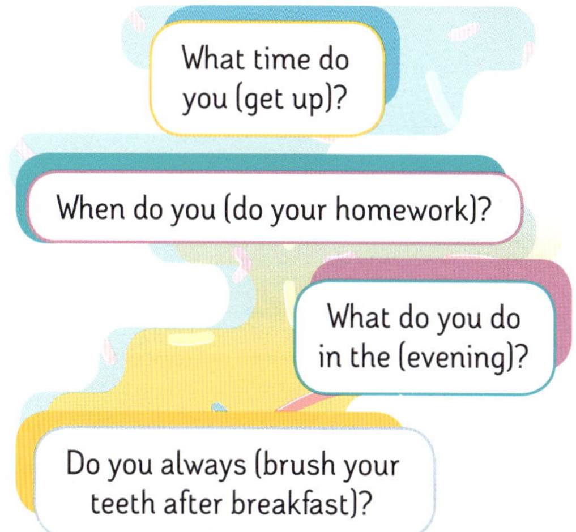

Study Space

5 **Return to your timeline in activity 2 on page 104. Include other activities you usually do.**

6 **Using the activities on the timeline on page 104, plan a presentation about your daily routine.**

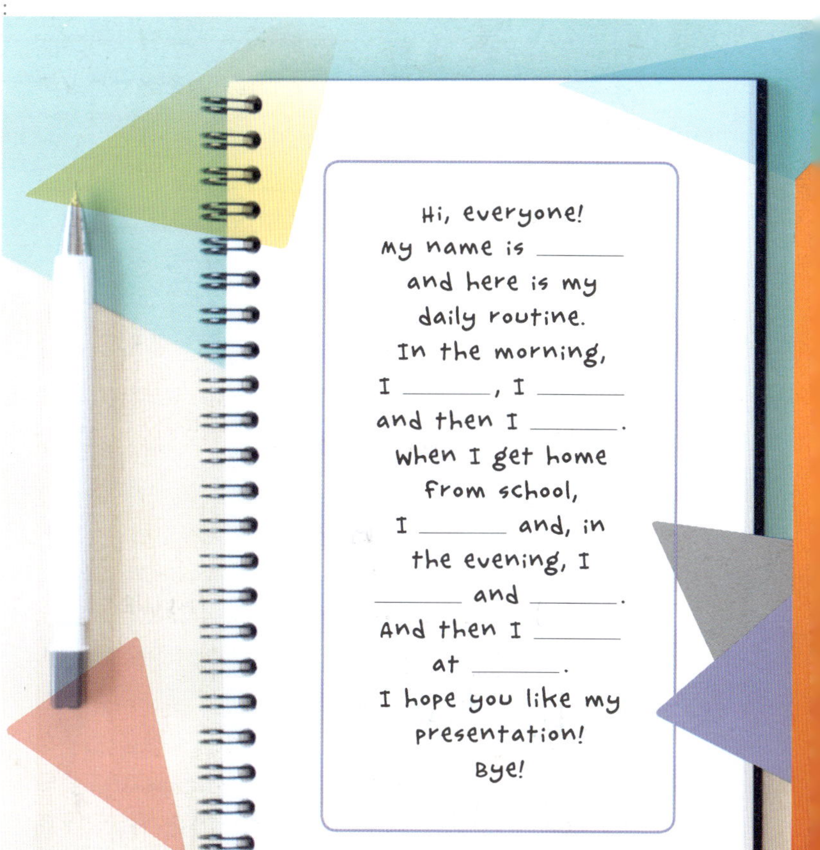

7 **Make a video of your presentation and share it on #MAKERS Digital <www.richmondmakers.com>. Use the hashtag #MyDailyRoutine.**

READING

Before Reading

1 Analyze the image below and discuss the following questions.

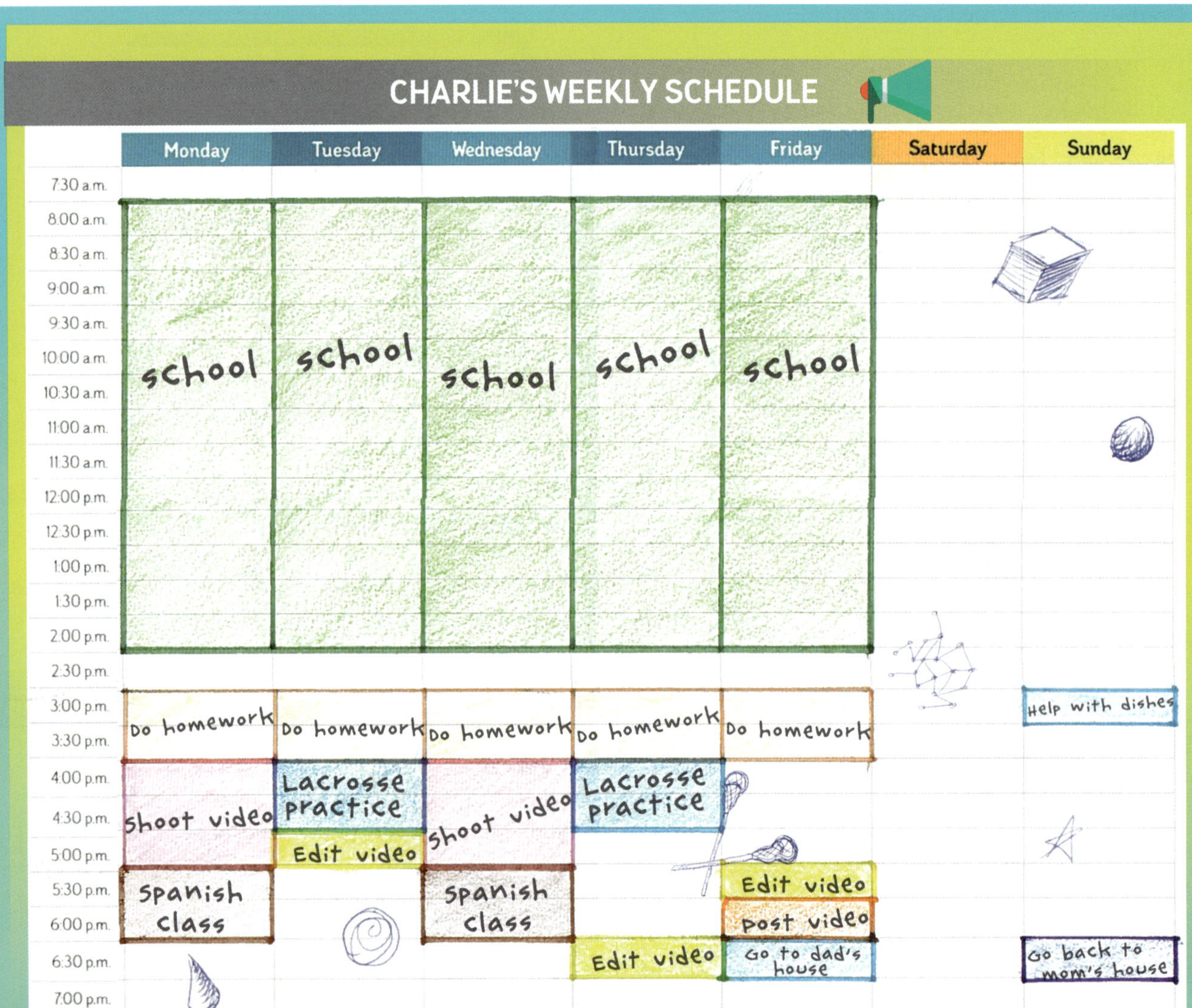

CHARLIE SIMMONS

Charlie Simmons is a 16-year-old student from Pasadena, California, who has over 100 thousand followers on his online channel, where he posts challenge videos, funny skits and videos about his life. Because of school and his video channel, Charlie is very busy. He needs to study, shoot and edit his videos and do sports. How does he do all that?

Charlie is in high school, so he wakes up at 6:30 a.m. Then he brushes his teeth and goes to school by bus with his sister. He doesn't have breakfast at home because he eats a snack when he arrives at school. After school, he does homework, reads magazines or books, shoots and edits videos for his channel and posts his videos every Friday. He practices lacrosse on Tuesdays and Thursdays afternoons, has Spanish classes on Mondays and Wednesdays and on Friday evenings he goes to his dad's house. After all that, he likes to unwind: he takes a shower, watches TV and plays video games before he goes to bed.

1 What kind of text is this?

2 Where can you find this kind of text?

3 Why do people use this kind of text?

4 What are some characteristics of these texts?

While Reading

2 **Who's Charlie? Look at the images and check.**

a 

b 

c 

3 **Read Charlie's weekly schedule and answer.**

1 When does Charlie...

a practice lacrosse?

____

b do his homework?

____

____

c post his videos?

____

d go to his dad's house?

____

e help with the dishes?

____

2 How long does Charlie spend shooting and editing his videos in a week?

____

4 **Read the article about Charlie and write T (true) or F (false). Then correct the false statements.**

1 ☐ Charlie is from New York.

____

2 ☐ His online video channel has more than 100,000 followers.

____

3 ☐ He goes to school alone.

____

4 ☐ He has breakfast at school.

____

5 ☐ He likes to play video games to relax.

____

5 **After reading the text, what can we infer about Charlie's family? Circle the correct options.**

1 Charlie's parents **live** / **don't live** together.

2 Charlie lives with his **mom** / **dad** during the week.

3 Charlie's sister **lives** / **doesn't live** with him during the week.

4 It's **possible** / **not possible** to say if Charlie has more siblings.

Study Space

After Reading

6 **Do you think making a weekly schedule is a good way to get organized? Why? What do you do to be more organized?**

Buzzwords

*"After all that, he likes to **unwind**."*
What does "unwind" mean in this context? Look it up!

7 **What do you do to unwind?**

____

____

____

____

____

____

Workbook p. 151

LANGUAGE 2

1 Compare the pairs of sentences below and discuss the differences between them.

1 I wake up at 6:30.
Charlie wakes up at 6:30.

2 I don't have breakfast at home.
He doesn't have breakfast at home.

3 How do you go to school?
How does he go to school?

Simple Present: 3rd Person Singular

Affirmative

Charlie **posts** challenge videos.
His online video channel **has** over 100,000 followers.

Negative

He **doesn't have** breakfast at home.
My sister **doesn't wash** her hair in the morning.

Interrogative

How does he do all that?
Who does Charlie go to school with?
Does Charlie like Math?

Short Answers

Yes, he does.
No, he doesn't.

2 Write questions using the prompts below.

1 she / go / to Italy / in the summer
______

2 what time / the movie / start
______

3 he / like / to play / baseball
______

4 when / Harry / want / to leave
______

5 who / Hanna / have lunch with
______

6 how / your brother / go / to the beach
______

7 does / he / brush his teeth / after dinner
______

3 Complete the sentences about a girl's routine with the correct form of the verbs in parentheses.

1 Zoey ______ (wake up) at 6 a.m.

2 She ______ (brush) her teeth in the morning.

3 She ______ (not / go) to school in the morning.

4 She ______ (go) to school by bus at 12:30 p.m.

5 She ______ (not / have) lunch at school.

6 She ______ (play) tennis on Mondays, Wednesdays and Fridays.

7 She ______ (do) her homework in the evening.

8 She ______ (have) dinner after she ______ (finish) her homework.

4 Match the questions to the answers.

1 Is the Earth flat?
2 Does the sun rise in the east?
3 Are clouds made of smoke?
4 Does the Earth revolve around the moon?
5 Do active volcanoes erupt?
6 Is the moon a satellite?
7 Are whales mammals?

a [ ] No, they aren't.
b [ ] Yes, they do.
c [ ] Yes, it does.
d [ ] No, it isn't.
e [ ] No, it doesn't.
f [ ] Yes, they are.
g [ ] Yes, it is.

Study Space

Snack Learning

Means of Transportation

by bike / boat / bus / car / plane / subway / train

on foot

5 Look at the images and complete the sentences with the verb to go in the affirmative or negative form.

1

Jenny ________ to school by car.

2

My best friends ________ home by bus.

3

My brother ________ to the park on foot.

4

I ________ to my cousin's house by plane.

5

Larry ________ to the beach by subway.

6 Rewrite the negative sentences from activity 5 to make them true according to the images.

1 ____________________

2 ____________________

3 ____________________

7 Complete the sentences so that they are true for you.

1 I go to school ____________.

2 My friends usually go to school ____________.

3 My parents go to work ____________.

4 I go to my friends' house ____________.

5 My grandparents come to my house ____________.

6 During vacation we usually travel ____________.

Study Space

Pronunciation

8 48 Listen to the sentences and write down the verbs used in each one.

1 ________ 5 ________

2 ________ 6 ________

3 ________ 7 ________

4 ________ 8 ________

9 49 Listen to the verbs again and classify them according to their pronunciation.

/s/	/z/	/ɪz/

10 50 Listen to the sentences from activity 8 again and practice.

11 Ask and answer questions with a classmate. Then report your findings to the rest of the class.

1 Do you...?

2 What do you...?

3 When do you...?

4 How do you...?

5 Who do you...?

Workbook p. 151

WRITING

A Weekly Schedule

Before Writing

1 **Plan your text. Think about all of the tasks you need to do in a week and answer the question.**

- What are your tasks in a typical week? Make a list.

Drafting

2 **Write a draft.**

3 **Share your draft with a classmate and ask for his/her opinion. Make adjustments, if necessary.**

Final Writing

4 **Write the final version of your weekly schedule and publish it on #MAKERS Digital <www.richmondmakers.com>. Use the hashtag #MyWeeklySchedule.**

Makerspace p. 117

INVESTIGATE

no little a lot of

I have __________ free time.

Collect Data

- Monitor your activities during a week by writing in your notebook the beginning and ending time of everything you do before and after school.

Analyze the Data

- How many hours a week do you spend doing your homework?
- How many hours a week do you spend doing school-related activities?
- How many hours a week do you spend doing household chores?
- Do you have time to do things for fun on weekdays?
- How many hours a week do you spend on your cell phone?
- How many hours a week do you spend playing sports?
- How many hours a week do you spend doing leisure activities?

Draw a Conclusion

I have __________ free time.

1 **Reflect on your conclusion and discuss the following questions.**

1. Why do you think you have no/little/a lot of free time?
2. Do you think having that much free time is good or bad? Why?
3. Do you think you need to change some things in your routine? If so, what?
4. In your opinion, what are the positive and negative aspects of having a lot of free time?
5. What can be the advantages and disadvantages of having little free time?

2 **Share your ideas on #MAKERS Digital <www.richmondmakers.com>. Use the hashtag #MyFreeTime.**

REVIEW 8

1 **Unscramble the letters and write the routine activities.**

1 VHEA UCNHL

____

2 TEG OEHM

____

3 UHBSR YM ETTHE

____

4 KTEA A OSHERW

____

5 VEAH IDNERN

____

6 OG OT CSOOHL

____

7 TEG PU

____

8 OD YM HWRKOEMO

____

9 HVEA FRAEBKSAT

____

10 OG OT DBE

____

11 KEAT ETH BSU

____

12 GTE DSEEDRS

____

2 **Complete the text using the expressions from activity 1.**

I (1) ______________ at 6 a.m. every day. The first thing I do in the morning is (2) ______________ and then I (3) ______________ with my mom. After that, I (4) ______________ and (5) ______________ at 7:30 a.m. to (6) ______________. I (7) ______________ at school every day and my classes end at 3 p.m. When I (8) ______________, I (9) ______________ and play video games until I (10) ______________. Then I (11) ______________ with my family, watch TV and (12) ______________ at about 9:30 p.m.

3 **Complete the sentences about Kim's routine with the correct form of the verbs in parentheses.**

1 Kim ______________ (go) to school in the afternoon.

2 She ______________ (have) dance classes on Fridays.

3 She ______________ (not / do) her homework in the evening.

4 She ______________ (walk) her dog every Saturday.

5 She ______________ (not / take) the bus to school.

4 **Match the questions to the answers.**

1 How does Eric go to school?

2 Does he have breakfast every morning?

3 When does he watch TV?

4 What does he do in the afternoon?

5 What time does he do his homework?

6 Who does he go to school with?

a [ ] No, he doesn't.

b [ ] At 9:30 a.m.

c [ ] He has classes at school.

d [ ] By car.

e [ ] His brother.

f [ ] In the evening.

5 **Cross out the mistakes and rewrite the sentences correcting them.**

1 Alfred ~~live~~ in Glasgow.
Alfred lives in Glasgow.

2 Do Tony have a salad for lunch?

____

3 David don't play sports.

____

4 Fred do his homework after school.

____

5 When Simone studies Spanish?

____

6 Karina doesn't watches TV in the evening.

____

Makerspace Unit 3 Building a Crate Shelf

Basic Supplies

acrylic paint and brushes

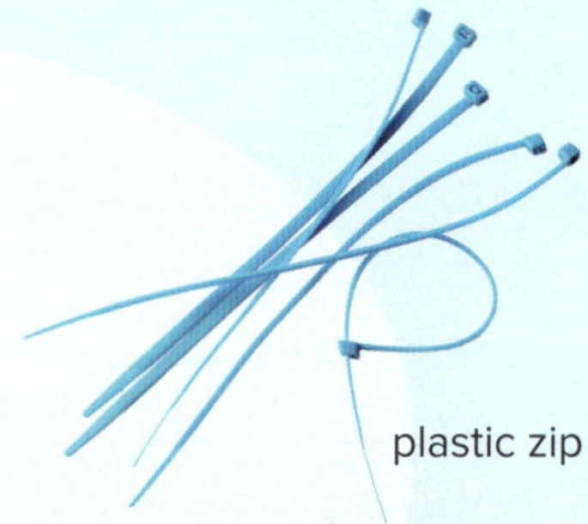

plastic zip ties

sandpaper

wooden crates

tape measure

Action

1 Look around the classroom and decide where would be a good place to have a shelf in order to organize the school materials you and your classmates have.

2 Use a tape measure to measure the space you have for the shelf.

3 Search online for crate shelves to get some inspiration.

4 Decide on the size, design and color (or colors) of the shelf.

5 Arrange the basic materials.

Problem-solving

- Are there enough crates for the design you have in mind? If not, are you going to get more crates or are you going to adapt the design of the shelf?
- Are all crates the same size and shape? If not, is that a problem? What do you need to adjust?

6 In groups, decide on how each student is going to help in the process.

7 Use the sandpaper to make the crates smooth so that no one gets hurt.

8 Apply one coat of paint to the crates and let them dry. Then apply more coats of paint as necessary.

9 Use the plastic zip ties to secure the crates together.

Problem-solving

- Are you going to keep heavy objects on the shelf? Is it safer to attach it to the wall? If so, are you going to use hook-and-loop fasteners, L brackets or something else? What other possibilities are there?
- Which factors do you need to take into consideration when thinking about how to attach your shelf to the wall?
- Who can help you attach the shelf to the wall?

10 Assemble the shelf in its location.

11 Organize on the shelf the materials you and your classmates have.

Assessment

- Did your shelf turn out the way you imagined it?
- Did it help organize the materials you and your classmates have?
- Did you have any problems that you couldn't solve?
- Will you do anything differently if you build another piece of furniture in the future?

Unit 6 Building a Sign for School

Basic Supplies

brush and acrylic paint

sandpaper

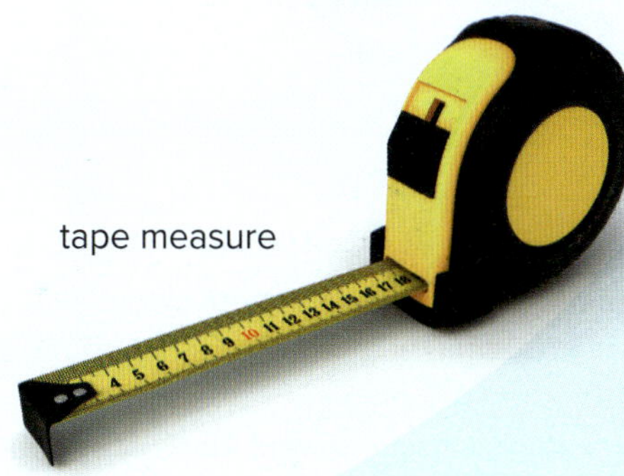

tape measure

piece of wood from demolition waste

Action

1 Go back to page 84 and review your answers for the questions in the **Before Writing** subsection.
2 Search online for "handmade signs" to get inspired.
3 Decide on the shape and size of the sign.
4 Decide on the colors of the sign (background and lettering).
5 Arrange the basic materials.
6 Use a tape measure to measure the space you have for the sign.

Problem-solving

- Is the sign going to stay outdoors? If so, what do you need to protect it from the sun and rain?
- Is your sign going to be attached to a pole? Or is it going to be hanging or leaning on the wall? In either case, what other materials do you need?
- Does the piece of wood you got correspond to the shape you want? If not, what do you need to change it?

7 Use the sandpaper to make the piece of wood smoother.
8 Apply one coat of paint to the sign and let it dry.
9 Apply more coats of paint as necessary.

Problem-solving

- How are you going to write the text on the sign? Are you going to write it in pencil first and then paint it? Or are you going to transfer it using a stencil? What other possibilities are there?

10 Write the text on the sign and let the paint dry.
11 Place your sign at the chosen location.

Assessment

- Does your sign look the way you imagined it?
- Did you have any problems that you couldn't solve?
- Will you do anything differently if you build another sign?

Makerspace Unit 7 Starting a New School Club

Basic Supplies

a computer

a printer

poster paper

markers

sheets of paper

Action

1 Go back to page 98 and review your answers for activity 1 of the **Draw a Conclusion** subsection.

2 Look for information about school clubs. Find out what a school club is, what its objectives are and how it works.

3 In groups, think about different kinds of school clubs that allow students to take part in individual and group activities. In a book club, for example, members read books individually first, but then discuss their impressions and ideas collectively.

4 Decide what kind of school club you would like to start.

5 Choose one or two representatives to talk to the school principal about the possibility of starting your club. Remember to find out if there is a vacant room where you can hold club meetings and make sure the school does not already have a similar club.

Problem-solving

- If there is no vacant room, where could the club meet? In your own classroom after classes or during breaks? On the school patio?
- If the school already has a similar club, what other club would you be interested in starting?

6 In the same groups, define the club's name, its purpose, the activities members will take part in and the goals you want the club to achieve. Decide also how often the club will meet, who will be allowed to join it and how the recruiting process will work.

Problem-solving

- Will anyone be allowed to join the club? If not, will potential members need to try out for the club?
- Will students have to sign up for the club? If so, where will the list be available?

7 Come up with the club's proposal. Choose someone to type it up and make the necessary adjustments. Then print out a copy to give to the principal.

8 Choose a couple of representatives to talk to the principal and register your club. Be prepared to answer his/her questions about it.

9 Choose a teacher or another staff member to be the club supervisor. Decide who will invite him/her to play this role and what his/her responsibilities will be.

10 Create posters and flyers to advertise the club. In smaller groups, plan the content and layout of these materials, as well as where they will be placed or handed out. Remember to include the following information: club name; objectives; place, day and time of the meetings; recruiting process; invitation for the first meeting. Then display the posters and distribute the flyers.

11 Hold your first club meeting and assign leadership roles (president, vice-president, secretary and treasurer). Remember to choose how communication between club members will take place.

12 Keep your school club going. Plan events that members enjoy and encourage them to voice their ideas and contribute to the success of the club. Keep spreading the word and recruiting new members.

Assessment

- Did your school club turn out the way you imagined it?
- Did you face any problems that you couldn't solve?
- Could you meet the goals you set for the club?
- Did your club promote both individual and group activities?
- Will you do anything differently if you start another school club in the future?

Unit 8 Creating a Bullet Journal

Basic Supplies

markers

pens and colored pencils

notebook (or notepad)

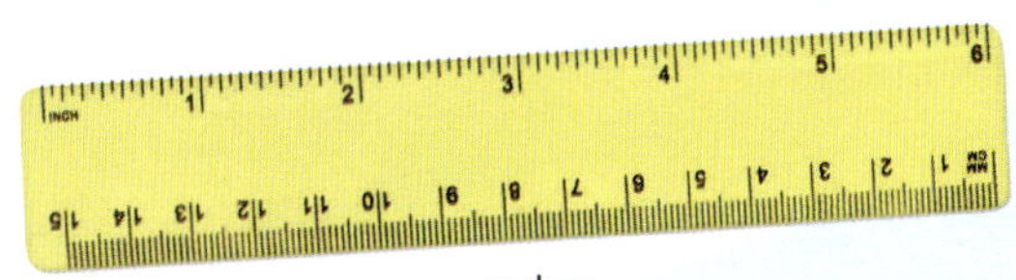

ruler

Action

1 Research online about bullet journals and find out what they are, what the purpose of using them is and how you can make one.

2 Find out people you know who use a bullet journal and ask them how they use it and what for.

3 Select some images of bullet journals to use as inspiration.

Problem-solving

- Analyze the images you selected. What other materials (besides the ones listed above) do you want to use?
- Are these materials easy to find? Are they affordable?

4 Arrange the materials for your bullet journal.

5 Decide which symbols you want to use.

Problem-solving

- What kind of information do you want to include in your journal?
- How can you distinguish the different types of information?
- How can you make sure you don't forget the symbols you chose and what they mean?

6 Look at the weekly schedule you wrote in the **Writing** session and your findings in the **Investigate** session (page 110). Use this information to write your bullet journal.

Problem-solving

- Where are you going to write a weekly schedule on your bullet journal: right at the beginning, at the end or somewhere else?
- How can you make it easier to read your weekly schedule? Can you use colors?

7 Using a ruler, separate a slot in your bullet journal for each day of the month or for each week.

Problem-solving

- Do you usually write a lot or do you prefer to use very short sentences? How does that affect the size of the spaces you need to separate for each day?
- Do the slots for every day of the week need to have the same space for you to write on? If not, what days need more or less space?

8 Fill in the days with events, appointments, deadlines etc. Use the symbols you have chosen in step 5.

9 Add other sections to your bullet journal based on your interests: movies you want to see, concerts you wish to attend etc.

Assessment

- Did your bullet journal turn out the way you imagined it?
- Did you face any problems that you couldn't solve?
- Do you think it will help you be more organized? How?
- Will you do anything differently if you create another bullet journal? If so, what?

Language Reference Units 1 and 2

▶ Verb to Be

Affirmative			Negative			Interrogative			Short Answers
I	am/'m	11 years old.	I	am not/'m not	Nigerian.	Am	I	from Canada?	Yes, I am. / No, I'm not.
You	are/'re		You	are not/aren't		Are	you		Yes, you are. / No, you aren't.
He	is/'s		He	is not/isn't		Is	he		Yes, he is. / No, he isn't.
She			She				she		Yes, she is. / No, she isn't.
It			It				it		Yes, it is. / No, it isn't.
We	are/'re		We	are not/aren't		Are	we		Yes, we are. / No, we aren't.
You			You				you		Yes, you are. / No, you aren't.
They			They				they		Yes, they are. / No, they aren't.

The verb to be is used to **describe a state or a characteristic.**

1 Read the text and check the correct options to complete it.

My name (1) ______ Justine.
I (2) ______ 13 years old. My birthday (3) ______ in August. I (4) ______ French. I (5) ______ from a small city called Nice. I have two sisters. Their names (6) ______ Angelique and Annette. They (7) ______ 20 years old. They love music. Angelique (8) ______ a pianist and Annette (9) ______ a singer.
Their favorite artist (10) ______ Adele.

1 ☐ am ☐ is ☐ are
2 ☐ am ☐ is ☐ are
3 ☐ am ☐ is ☐ are
4 ☐ am ☐ is ☐ are
5 ☐ am ☐ is ☐ are
6 ☐ am ☐ is ☐ are
7 ☐ am ☐ is ☐ are
8 ☐ am ☐ is ☐ are
9 ☐ am ☐ is ☐ are
10 ☐ am ☐ is ☐ are

2 Read the dialogue and circle the correct options to complete it.

Lily: Good morning, Jake! How (1) **are** / **am** you?

Jake: Hi, Lily! I (2) **'s** / **'m** fine. What about you? (3) **Is** / **Are** you OK?

Lily: Yes, I (4) **am** / **am not**.

Jake: Let me see my schedule... It (5) **'re** / **'s** Monday, so I have Science now. It (6) **'s** / **isn't** my favorite subject, I love it! What about you?

Lily: I have History now, but it (7) **is** / **isn't** my favorite subject. My favorite subject (8) **is** / **isn't** Science too.

Jake: (9) **Am** / **Is** your teacher Mrs. Campbell?

Lily: No, it (10) **is** / **isn't**. It (11) **'s** / **isn't** Mr. Blake. (12) **Are** / **Is** Mrs. Campbell a good teacher?

Jake: Yes, she (13) **is** / **isn't**. Her classes (14) **are** / **is** really interesting!

Lily: Oops, the bell! Listen, do you want to go to the park after school? It (15) **is** / **isn't** too cold today, so we can play soccer.

Jake: Great idea, let's go!

Lily: Deal! See you after class!

Jake: Bye!

Demonstrative Pronouns

This is my phone.

These are my books.

That is my T-shirt.

Those are my apples.

This and ***these*** are used to refer to things that are **close** to the speaker. ***That*** and ***those*** are used to refer to things that are **far** from the speaker. ***This*** and ***that*** are used to refer to **singular** things. ***These*** and ***those*** are used to refer to **plural** things.

3 Complete the sentences with *this*, *that*, *these* or *those*.

1 Are ________________ pens in the box here yours?

2 ________________ building on the next block is the Empire State Building.

3 Look at ________________ book here. It looks very interesting!

4 ________________ are my parents over there. Can you see them, near the pool?

4 Put the words in the correct order to make sentences.

1 a / this / car / German / not / is / .

____

2 Camila / that / my / is / friend / .

____

3 great / sandwiches / those / are / .

____

4 from / bananas / Florida / these / are / ?

____

5 my / are / pencils / not / these / .

____

6 boys / are / those / cousins / your / ?

____

7 girl / from / that / England / is / ?

____

5 Rewrite the sentences in the plural.

1 This is my orange.

____

2 This isn't my book.

____

3 That is his pen.

____

4 Is that your video game?

____

6 Look at the images and write sentences to describe them. Use *this*, *that*, *these* or *those*.

1

2

3

4

1 ________________

2 ________________

3 ________________

4 ________________

Unit 3

Plural Nouns

For most of the words, we just add **-s** to form the plural.
I have only one pen, but my sister has many pen**s**.
I want to eat a banana, but my friend wants to eat two banana**s**.

If a word ends in **ch**, **s**, **sh**, **x** or **z**, we add **-es** to form the plural.
My cousin has one watch, but I have five watch**es**.
This is a small bus, but those are very big bus**es**.
My mom is carrying one box, but I'm carrying two box**es**.

If a word ends in **y** and the letter before it is a **vowel**, we just add **-s** to form the plural.

I see only one boy in the swimming pool, but there are four boy**s** on the swimming team.
This is my brother's favorite toy, but he likes all his toy**s**.

If a word ends in **y** and the letter before it is a **consonant**, we drop the **y** and add **-ies**.
There is a big library at school and in my neighborhood there are three librar**ies**.
My mom has a baby, but my aunt has two bab**ies**: they're twins.

1 **Check the correct plural form to complete the sentences.**

1 My ______ are yellow.
a ☐ toothbrushs b ☒ toothbrushes

2 I want to buy some ______.
a ☒ peaches b ☐ peach

3 I have two ______ to go to on Saturday.
a ☒ parties b ☐ partys

4 My cousin has two ______.
a ☒ ponies b ☐ ponys

5 The ______ in the cafeteria are white.
a ☐ tableses b ☒ tables

2 **Rewrite the sentences in the plural.**

1 This is a green car.
These are green cars.

2 I have a dictionary.
I have dictionaries

3 He is an astronaut.
They are astronauts

4 Is that a fox?
Are those foxes?

5 The boy is a student.
These boys are students

There to Be

Affirmative			Negative			Interrogative			Short Answers
There	is/'s	a black car on the street.	There	is not/ isn't	an Australian book in the library.	Is	there	a museum nearby?	Yes, there is. / No, there isn't.
There	are	two black cars on the street.	There	are not/ aren't	many Australian books in the library.	Are	there	any museums nearby?	Yes, there are. / No, there aren't.

The structure ***there* + verb to be** is used to say that something **exists**.
We use ***there is*/*there's*** to talk about **one element** and ***there are*** to talk about **two or more elements**.

3 Read the sentences and check the best option to complete them.

1 **A:** ______ a lot of students in your class?
B: No, ______.
a Are there / is there
b Are there / there aren't
c Is there / there is

2 ______ a laptop on my desk.
a There are
b There isn't
c Is there

3 **A:** ______ a supermarket near here?
B: Yes, ______.
a Are there / is there
b There is / there are
c Is there / there is

4 ______ a book in my backpack.
a There is
b There are
c Is there

5 ______ two auditoriums in my sister's school.
a There isn't
b Are there
c There are

6 **A:** ______ five books in your locker?
B: No, ______. ______ only two books there.
a Are there / there are / There are
b Are there / there aren't / There are
c There are / there aren't / Are there

4 Complete the sentences using there to be in the correct form.

1 ______ eight planets in the solar system.
2 ______ seven colors in the rainbow?
3 ______ four sides in a triangle.
4 How many students ______ in your school?
5 ______ more than one continent named Europe in the world.
6 ______ twelve months in a year.
7 ______ a swimming pool in your school?
8 ______ a country named Liechtenstein in Europe.

A/An

This is **a** banana.

This is **a** car.
They live in **a** really big house.
That is **a** uniform.

This is **an** egg.

That is **an** apple.
This is **an** eraser.
I want **an** orange pencil.

Use indefinite articles ***a*** and ***an*** before **singular nouns**. Use ***a*** before words that start with a **consonant sound** and ***an*** before words that start with a **vowel sound**.

5 Circle the correct options to complete the sentences.

1 I have **a** / **an** / – orange bike.

2 **A:** What's this?
B: It's **a** / **an** / – dictionary.

3 **A:** Do you like this book?
B: Oh, I love it! It's **a** / **an** / – excellent book.

4 These are **a** / **an** / – beautiful uniforms.

5 Are those **a** / **an** / – apples? I want some.

6 There are 365 days in **a** / **an** / – year.

7 **A:** What's in that building?
B: There's **a** / **an** / – university there.

Prepositions of Place

Prepositions of place are used to describe **where something or someone is** in relation to something/ someone else.

6 Look at the images and write sentences about where things are. Use there to be and the appropriate articles.

a There are apples in the box.
b There is a box on the table.

a ______ trees ______ the house.
b ______ house ______ the trees.

a ______ glass of juice ______ the sandwich.
b ______ egg ______ the sandwich.

a ______ plate ______ the fork and the knife.
b ______ purple napkin ______ the plate.

Unit 4

▶ Possessive Adjectives

Subject Pronoun	Possessive Adjective	Example
I	my	I like **my** car.
you	your	Peter, is this **your** cat?
he	his	This is Robert and **his** brother.
she	her	This is my mother and that is **her** sister.
it	its	Look at that bird. **Its** wings are brown.
we	our	My cousins and I love **our** grandmother.
you	your	You and Maria have five brothers. **Your** family is big!
they	their	My parents are the best! **Their** names are Mark and Natalie.

Possessive adjectives are used to indicate that something **belongs** to someone.

1 Rewrite the sentences using possessive adjectives.

1 This book belongs to me.
This is my book.

2 That house belongs to you and me.
____

3 That notebook belongs to Philip.
____

4 Those toys belong to Mary and Sally.
____

5 This sandwich belongs to you.
____

6 This ball belongs to that cat over there.
____

7 That bed belongs to Pamela.
____

2 Circle the correct option to complete the sentences.

1 Mike and Tina love music. **Her** / **Their** favorite band is U2.

2 Are you a new student? What's **your** / **our** name?

3 Australia is a big country. **Its** / **His** capital is Canberra.

4 Mrs. Black is our teacher. **His** / **Her** birthday is in September.

5 My friend and I are British, but **my** / **our** parents are from the U.S.

6 My dad is from Colombia. **His** / **Its** name is Pedro.

3 Complete the sentences using the words from the box.

her	his	I	its	my	our
she	their	they	you	your	

1 The newspaper is publishing _______ first digital edition.

2 _______ pets are great! _______ love them!

3 Mark loves fruit and _______ favorite dessert is fruit salad.

4 This is Sheila's backpack. _______ always forgets _______ backpack here!

5 Sean and I are looking for _______ books, but we can't find them anywhere.

6 Diana and William are not done with _______ homework because _______ can't understand the last activity.

7 Hey, everyone, _______ can have _______ snacks now, it's time for the break.

4 Complete the sentences using the correct possessive adjective.

1 This is my sister. _______ name is Joanne.

2 Wow, look at that turtle eating! _______ favorite food seems to be carrots!

3 Maya and Mike are my cousins. _______ house is next to my school.

4 My neighbor Lukasz is from Poland and _______ father, Krzysztof, is from Poland too.

Genitive Case

This is Camille's laptop.

Baseball is Janet's favorite sport.

We use the **genitive case** to express that something **belongs** to someone else, something else or a group of people (a team, for example).

With singular nouns, we add **'s** to the noun that indicates the owner.

Jake's car is yellow.

Mark's pen is new.

With plural nouns ending in **s**, we just add **'** to the noun that indicates the owner.

The doctors' opinions are different.

The teachers' lockers are down the hall.

With plural nouns not ending in **s**, we add **'s** to the noun that indicates the owner.

They are discussing women's tasks in the company.

The children's toys are in the living room.

If a singular noun ends in **s**, we add **'s** to the noun that indicates the owner. However, if it is a classical or religious name, we just add **'** to the noun that indicates the owner.

Frances's burgers are delicious!

Sophocles' plays still have many fans.

When a single thing belongs to two or more different people, we add **'** to the last noun that indicates the owner.

This is John and Jacob's brother. (John and Jacob have the same brother.)

Fran and Victor's house is in front of the bank. (Fran and Victor live in the same house.)

When two or more things belong to two or more different owners, we add **'s** to every noun that indicates a different owner.

These are John's and Jacob's bikes. (John has a bike and Jacob has another bike.)

Fran's and Victor's houses are in front of the bank. (Fran lives in a house and Victor lives in a different house.)

5 **Rewrite the sentences using the genitive case.**

1 This car belongs to Romeo.

____

2 This pen belongs to Peter and this other pen belongs to Parker.

____

3 This book belongs to Agnes.

____

4 This park belongs to the people.

____

5 These cards belong to Mary and Sally.

____

6 That project belongs to the students.

____

6 **Read the sentences and find the mistakes. Then cross them out and rewrite the sentences correcting them.**

1 These are the boys's pencils.

____

2 This is Zoey' bike.

____

3 The children' beds are new.

____

4 Susan's and Steve school is old.

____

5 Parents' Scott are from New Zealand.

____

7 **Check the correct option to complete the sentences.**

1 Our cousins _______ cars are in the garage.

a ☐ 's b ☐ ' c ☐ –

2 There are lots of students _______ in my school.

a ☐ 's b ☐ ' c ☐ –

3 The restaurant _______ delivery service is closed today.

a ☐ 's b ☐ ' c ☐ –

4 My parents _______ phones are new, but Lucas _______ phone is old.

a ☐ 's / ' b ☐ ' / 's c ☐ – / 's

Unit 5

Present Continuous

Affirmative		Negative		Interrogative			Short Answers
I	am/'m reading a magazine.	I	am not/'m not listening to music.	Am	I	drinking water?	Yes, I am. / No, I'm not.
You	are/'re watching TV.	You	are not/aren't doing your homework.	Are	you		Yes, you are. / No, you aren't.
He	is/'s sleeping.	He	is not/isn't eating.	Is	he		Yes, he is. / No, he isn't.
She		She			she		Yes, she is. / No, she isn't.
It		It			it		Yes, it is. / No, it isn't.
We	are/'re working.	We	are not/aren't having Science classes.	Are	we		Yes, we are. / No, we aren't.
You		You			you		Yes, you are. / No, you aren't.
They		They			they		Yes, they are. / No, they aren't.

The **present continuous** is used to describe an **action that is happening at the moment of speaking**.

Usually, we just add ***-ing*** to the main verb (the verb that describes the action and comes after the verb to be).
I'm drink**ing** orange juice.
They're eat**ing** an apple pie.

If the main verb ends in **e**, we drop the **e** and add ***-ing***.
We are tak**ing** the bus to go downtown.
She is mak**ing** a sandwich.

If the main verb ends in **consonant-vowel-consonant** and the last syllable is stressed, we double the final consonant and add ***-ing***.
Is he swim**ming** right now?
The cat isn't run**ning**.

1 Underline the correct options to complete the dialogue.

Zoey: Hey, Logan. What's up?

Logan: Nothing much. What (1) **are you doing / doing you**?

Zoey: I (2) **am watch / 'm watching** a movie on TV, actually.

Logan: Really? Is it good?

Zoey: Yeah, it seems pretty good. I'm in the middle of this big action scene. Some guys (3) **are tring / are trying** to rob a bank, but a woman sees it and right now she (4) **isn't calling / is calling** the police. She (5) **isn't shouting / aren't shouting** or anything, so nobody knows what she (6) **is do / 's doing**. Oh, the police officers (7) **are going / aren't go** to the bank.

Logan: Are they (8) **geting / getting** their cars?

Zoey: Yes, they (9) **are / aren't**. Now they (10) **are chasing / are chassing** the robbers and everyone (11) **is runing / is running**.

Logan: Are the officers (12) **shooting / shootting**?

Zoey: No, they (13) **are / aren't**. Oh, wait! Now the robbers (14) **aren't shootting / are shooting**! People on the street are scared, so they (15) **are hiding / are hideing** behind cars. The stores (16) **are closing / are closeing** down and some children (17) **are cring / are crying**. A helicopter (18) **is fling / is flying** above the scene and the officers in it (19) **aren't trying / are trying** to see where the robbers (20) **aren't going / are going**. Oh, no! They (21) **are running / is runing** away! And they aren't leaving alone. They (22) **taking / 're taking** a hostage with them. Oh, no!

Logan: Are they (23) **hurtting / hurting** the hostage?

Zoey: No, they (24) **aren't / isn't**. They're getting in a car with all the money and the hostage and they're leaving.

Logan: Where (25) **are / am** they going?

Zoey: Oh, no! No, no, no, no!

Logan: What's (26) **go / going** on?

Zoey: The power went out. Now I can't finish watching the movie.

Logan: Oh, no! Now even I am curious to know what happens!

2 Order the words to make sentences.

1 in / sitting / yard / grandma / the / is

2 watching / we / on / movie / are / a / TV

3 is / at / sister / dinner / having / your / home

4 my / test / Science / are / the / studying / friends / for

5 are / rooms / boys / their / cleaning / the

3 What is happening? Look at the images and write sentences.

Let's + Verb

I am hungry. **Let's have** lunch!
It's very hot! **Let's open** the windows.
Judy is sick. **Let's visit** her at the hospital.

We use ***let's* + verb** to make **suggestions or invitations**.

4 **Look at the images. Then complete the dialogues with a suggestion from the box.**

Let's buy her a gift! | Let's drink some hot chocolate! | Let's go to the park! | Let's study together!

1

A: It's cold!
B: ____________________

2

A: It's my sister's birthday!
B: ____________________

3

A: We have a Math test tomorrow!
B: ____________________

4

A: I'm bored!
B: ____________________

Telling the Time

4:00 p.m. It's four **o'clock**.
4:15 p.m. It's **a quarter past** four p.m. / It's four fifteen p.m.
4:30 p.m. It's **half past** four p.m. / It's four thirty p.m.
4:45 p.m. It's **a quarter to** five p.m. / It's four forty-five p.m.

A: What time is it?
B: It's four thirty-eight p.m.

A: What time is it?
B: It's four twenty-two p.m.

5 **Match the images to the sentences.**

1

2

3

4

a [ ] It's eleven thirty a.m.
b [ ] It's a quarter past seven a.m.
c [ ] It's half past eleven p.m.
d [ ] It's a quarter to seven a.m.

Unit 6

Imperative

Open the window, it's a beautiful day outside.

Don't be upset, everything is going to be OK.

The **imperative** is used to **make requests and give suggestions, orders and instructions**.

1 Match the requests and orders to the school facilities.

1 Don't talk too loud.
2 Respect the line.
3 Don't dive.
4 Do activity 5 in pairs.
5 Wash your hands.

a [3] swimming pool
b [1] library
c [2] cafeteria
d [4] classroom
e [5] bathroom

2 Read sentences 1-5 in activity 1 again. Then find the imperative forms and write them down.

1 Don't talk
2 Respect
3 Don't dive
4 Do
5 Wash

3 Read the note and complete it with the verbs in parentheses in the imperative, either affirmative or negative.

Dear Lily,
I will be home late tonight, so I need you to take care of some things for me. (1) Take out (take out) the trash and (2) do (do) the dishes. (3) Don't use (use) the dishwasher, because it isn't working. (4) Pick up (pick up) your brother from swim practice and (5) give (give) him a snack. (6) do (do) your homework and (7) don't order (order) food for dinner, because there's pasta in the fridge. (8) Call (call) me if you need anything. See you later!
Love,
Mom

Units 7 and 8

Simple Present

Affirmative		Negative		Interrogative			Short Answers
I	**watch** TV in the evening.	I	**do not/don't play** video games.	**Do**	I		Yes, I do. / No, I don't.
You		You			you		Yes, you do. / No, you don't.
He	**wakes up** early.	He	**does not/doesn't drink** water in the morning.	**Does**	he	**go** to bed late?	Yes, he does. / No, he doesn't.
She		She			she		Yes, she does. / No, she doesn't.
It		It			it		Yes, it does. / No, it doesn't.
We	**have** lunch at school.	We	**do not/don't play** the piano.	**Do**	we		Yes, we do. / No, we don't.
You		You			you		Yes, you do. / No, you don't.
They		They			they		Yes, they do. / No, they don't.

The **simple present** is used to talk about **routines, habits, general truths and present states.**

Usually we just add **-s** to the main verb for third-person singular subjects.
He eat**s** pancakes for breakfast. My cat like**s** to sleep in the sun.

If the main verb ends in **sh**, **ch**, **s**, **x**, **z** or **o**, we add **-es** to the main verb for third-person singular subjects.
My dog go**es** to the park with us every Saturday. My cousin watch**es** TV in the evening.

If the main verb ends in **y** preceded by a **vowel**, we just add **-s** to the main verb for third-person singular subjects.
She play**s** the violin very well. My father buy**s** clothes twice a year.

If the main verb ends in **y** preceded by a **consonant**, we drop the **y** and add ***-ies*** to the main verb for third-person singular subjects.
My cousin always cr**ies** during movies. She usually stud**ies** in the afternoon.

The verb **to have** is irregular, so we use the form ***has*** for third-person singular subjects.
Mom **has** French lessons on Tuesdays and Thursdays. His brother **has** a new bike.

1 **Rewrite the sentences substituting the subject as indicated.**

1 I never try on new clothes in the store.
He ______.
2 They watch TV three times a week.
She ______.
3 We never stay in the same place.
My rabbit ______.
4 I get the bus to go to school.
My classmate ______
5 We sometimes fish in the lake.
He ______.
6 Airplanes fly really fast.
That airplane ______.
7 They usually pay for lunch in cash.
She ______.

2 **Complete the sentences using the verbs in parentheses.**

1 My mother ______ (go) to work by car.
2 They ______ (play) tennis after school.
3 We ______ (do) our homework in the evening.
4 Paul ______ (wake up) at 7 o'clock.
5 You ______ (speak) Russian fluently.
6 The book ______ (have) a wonderful ending.

3 **Rewrite the sentences from activity 2 in the negative form.**

1 ______
2 ______
3 ______
4 ______
5 ______
6 ______

4 Complete the dialogues about the sentences in activity 2 with either a question or an answer.

1 **A:** Does she go to work by car?
B: Yes, she does.

2 **A:** Do they play tennis before school?
B: No, they don't

3 **A:** Do you do your homework in the evening?
B: Yes, I we do

4 **A:** Doesn't Paul wake up at 7 o'clock
B: No, he doesn't.

5 **A:** Do you speak Russian fluently
B: Yes, I do.

6 **A:** Does the book have a terrible ending?
B: No, it doesn't

Expressing Frequency

100%	I **always** brush my teeth after meals. She is **always** happy.
	He **usually** eats cereal for breakfast. I am **usually** tired after school.
	They **often** play soccer on the weekend. He is **often** angry.
	We **sometimes** clean the house. We are **sometimes** sad.
0%	They **never** call me in the evening. I am **never** late for school.

Adverbs of frequency are used to say **how often something happens**.

They are placed **before the main verb** of the sentence. However, if the main verb is the **verb to be**, the adverb of frequency is placed **after it**.

Expressions of frequency are another way to say **how often something happens**.
Grandpa goes to the U.S. every August. He travels **once a year**.
Giulia studies German on Mondays and Wednesdays. She has classes **twice a week**.
Ryan goes to the dentist in April, August and December. He has dentist appointments **three times a year**.
I go to school from Monday to Friday. I have classes **five times a week**.
My dog eats at 10 a.m. and 7 p.m. He eats **twice a day**.

5 Look at Tiffany's activities during the week and make five sentences using the words from the box.

always never often sometimes usually

	MONDAY	TUESDAY	WEDNESDAY	THURSDAY	FRIDAY
study French		✓			✓
play the guitar			✓	✓	✓
do my homework	✓	✓	✓	✓	✓
call grandma	✓	✓	✓	✓	
go to sleep early					

1 Tiffany sometimes studies French.
2 Tiffany often plays the guitar
3 Tiffany always do my homework
4 Tiffany usually calls grandma
5 Tiffany never goes sleep early

6 Rewrite the sentences from activity 5 using expressions of frequency.

1 Tiffany studies French twice a week.
2 ______
3 ______
4 ______
5 ______

Means of Transportation

My parents go to the supermarket **by car**.
My cousin goes to college **by bus**.
Fred goes to the countryside **by train**.
My aunt goes to work **by subway**.
We go to Europe **by plane**.
I go to school **by bicycle**.
You go to your uncle's house **on foot**.

7 Look at the images and answer the questions.

1

A: How does Jim go to the park?
B: He goes to the park by bike.

2

A: How do they go to the beach?
B: ______

3

A: How does your aunt travel to Asia?
B: ______

4

A: How do we go to school?
B: ______

Question Words

A: **How often** do you talk to your mother?
B: I **always** talk to my mother. I talk to my mother **every day**.

A: **What** do you eat for lunch on Sundays?
B: I eat **spaghetti**.

A: **When** does she do her homework?
B: She does her homework **in the afternoon**.

A: **Who** plays the guitar well?
B: **Patrick** plays the guitar very well.

A: **How** do you go to school?
B: I go to school **by car**.

Question words are used to **ask about specific information**. ***How often*** is used to ask about **frequency**; ***what*** to ask about a **specific thing or action**; ***when*** to ask about **time**; ***who*** to ask about a **person**; and ***how*** to ask about the **way** something happens or somebody is or acts.

8 Complete the sentences below with a question word.

1 **A:** ______ do you want to buy for Ellen's birthday?
B: Some flowers.

2 **A:** ______ do you have volleyball practice?
B: On the weekend.

3 **A:** ______ do you usually go to Paris?
B: By train.

4 **A:** ______ is your favorite singer?
B: Taylor Swift.

5 **A:** ______ does Brian go to the movies?
B: Twice a month.

Making an Identity Collage

1 **Look at the images and discuss the questions in pairs.**

1. What do the images have in common? How are they different?
2. In your opinion, what is the purpose of images like these?
3. Which one do you like the most? Why?

2 **Read the steps below and follow your teacher's instructions.**

1. Search for images that represent you. They may include food you like, sports you are good at, places you like going to, your favorite books/movies/games/singers, words that are important to you etc. You can use your own pictures or cut-outs from magazines or newspapers. Remember not to include anything that contains your name or your face.
2. Decide on the design of your identity collage (size, format, number of images and words).
3. Cut the images out in different shapes and remember not to use the entire image, but only parts of it.
4. Make your identity collage.

3 **Display your collage in the classroom and look at your classmates' collages. Then try to guess who made each one.**

Unit 6 Traffic Day

1 Analyze the images and discuss.

1 What is wrong in each of these situations?

2 Do these situations (or other situations like these) happen where you live?

3 What do people have to do to prevent situations like these?

2 Get together in groups. Read the steps below and follow your teacher's instructions.

1 Select some traffic signs that are common in your region/country.

2 Prepare a memory game using these signs and their meanings.

3 Exchange memory games with another group and play it.

4 Make a list of traffic violations that are common in your region/country.

5 Make a "right and wrong" poster showing some of these violations.

6 Choose some violations and create a role-play.

7 Rehearse your role-play.

3 On Traffic Day, organize your station and present your work.

Glossary

WELCOME

candle a stick of wax that is burned to give light

cost the amount of money needed to buy something

doodle a drawing made distractedly

greeting a friendly word or gesture used to welcome or meet someone

hidden out of sight or difficult to find

meaning what a word, action, feeling or idea represents

missing not where it should be; absent

previous happening or appearing before something or someone else

speech bubble a graphic element in comics containing what a character says

speed how fast somebody or something moves

useful that can be used in a helpful, practical or effective way

wallet a small case to keep money, documents and cards

UNIT 1

capitalization the use of capital letters, instead of lower-case ones

country a piece of land where people live under the same government or have the same culture

draft first (unfinished) version of a text or a drawing

fictional imaginary; created for a book or film

field an area where information should be inserted

gymnastics physical exercises to develop agility, coordination and strength

heading the title at the beginning of a page or section

hurry up to move or do something more quickly

improve to make something better

nationality the condition of belonging to a country by being born there or becoming a citizen

nickname a familiar or informal name given to someone or something

purpose the reason why someone does something or something exists

share to publish content on social media so that other people can see it and react to it

statement something that someone says or writes expressing an opinion or idea

sticky note a piece of paper with an adhesive strip for notes and short messages

twin one of two children born at the same time that have the same mother

UNIT 2

allow to let someone do or have something; to permit

amazing very surprising in a positive way

average the resultant number you get by adding two or more quantities and then dividing the total by the number of quantities added

background elements behind the main people or things in pictures; previous experience or knowledge

building a construction that has a roof and walls

close not far in position or time; near

differ to be different from something or someone else

environment things and conditions that surround somebody or something

far distant; not near

hold to carry something or someone; to embrace someone

infer to conclude something based on information or evidence

joke a short story, usually with a funny ending, that is told to make people laugh

label a word or phrase used to describe somebody or something

matter to be important or relevant

near close; not far away

publish to make a text or image public; to print something in a book, magazine or other media

relative a member of someone's family

relevant connected with and important to what is happening or being discussed

replace to substitute; to put in the place of something or someone

research a detailed study of a subject to discover information and facts

spend to pass time doing something or being somewhere

UNIT 3

ad a notice about products, jobs, events or services; an advertisement

appeal the ability to attract interest and attention

assemble to bring together in a single place; to put together the parts of something

attach to connect something to something else

attractive able to gain the attention or admiration of others because of its appearance

backpack a bag that people use on their backs to carry things

basement the floor of a building below ground level

campaign activities planned for social, commercial or political purposes

coat a layer of a substance applied on a surface

convey to communicate a thought, idea or feeling

correction fluid a liquid substance applied to paper to mask errors in text

crate a box for packing, storing or shipping

criticize to indicate flaws or mistakes in a disapproving way

effective able to produce the desired result

gym a large room with special equipment designed to do physical exercises

heavy weighing a lot; difficult to lift or move

leaflet a piece of paper containing information or advertisement

locker a secure compartment where people put their possessions and leave them for a period of time

lucky having good luck; fortunate

odd strange; unusual

performance the act of presenting a play, concert or another form of entertainment

persuade to convince someone to do something through arguments

praise to express admiration or approval; to compliment

shape the physical form of something

shelf a flat board fixed horizontally against a wall on which objects are kept

size how large or small something or someone is

smooth having a surface with no holes, lumps or rough areas

successful achieving the desired result

theme the main subject of a piece of writing, talk or film

variety a number of different kinds of the same thing; a different type of something

wall vertical structure of a building that surrounds or divides an area

UNIT 4

alternate presenting a different possibility; substitute

amount the quantity of something

announce to make a formal statement about an event or intention

babysitter a person who looks after a baby or child while the parents are out

bathtub a container that is filled with water so that people can lie in it and wash their bodies

behave to act or do things in a certain way

billboard a large outdoor board for advertisements

break a short period of rest

comic strip a series of drawings in panels that tell an amusing story

dirty not clean

drawer a compartment that is part of a piece of furniture used for keeping objects and clothes

emphasize to give special importance or attention to something

furniture household or office articles used to make a room suitable or comfortable

guest a person who stays in someone's house or visits it

homelessness the state of having no place to live

open-plan a room with few or no walls

panel an individual frame in a comic strip

poor lacking money and possessions

properly in a satisfactory, correct way

raise to lift or move something to a higher level

strong powerful; very intense

teenager a young person aged between thirteen and nineteen years old

UNIT 5

bake to cook in an oven using dry heat at medium temperature

concert a musical performance for an audience

embarrassed feeling uncomfortable because of shame or from receiving too much attention

epic remarkable; incredible

face-to-face in person; facing directly

hang out to spend time with friends without any particular purpose

holiday a day of festivity on which most people do not work or study

implication consequence; what is likely to happen as a result

magazine a printed or online collection of stories, pictures, articles and advertisements

prevent to keep or stop something from happening

text to send someone a text message on a cell phone

UNIT 6

belong to be in the right place; to feel happy or comfortable in a particular place or environment

block an area of buildings with streets on each side

crowded full of people

description the process of saying what somebody or something is like

dry having no water in it

establishment a business organization or public institution

excerpt a short part of a film, music, text or book

gate a barrier similar to a door used to close an opening in a wall or fence

graffiti words or drawings on walls in public places

guide to direct or lead along a way that is not familiar

handmade made by a person instead of by a machine

lane one of the parts of a road divided by lines in order to keep vehicles or competitors separate

lean to stand at an angle against something for support

leash a strap or cord for restraining and guiding a dog

neighborhood a district or community in a city or town

pole a long stick used for holding or supporting things

polite behaving respectfully according to the usual rules of society

probable likely to happen

provide to make something available to someone

railing a fence made of metal or wood

regulatory used to inform about rules and regulations

request the act of asking politely for something

rubric a set of instructions

rule a law or direction that presents the required behavior or action

sign an object with words or images in it that provides information or advertises something

solve to find a solution to a problem

stencil a piece of cardboard, metal or plastic used to draw or paint patterns onto a surface

warning a sign that informs people about a possible danger or problem

wild living or growing in natural environments or conditions

UNIT 7

achieve to succeed in doing something or reaching a particular goal

advertise to announce something on media to sell or promote it

arch a structure with a curved top

assign to give somebody a job or a task to be done

buddy friend

chalk a stick of soft white rock used for writing or drawing

display to arrange something in a way that people can easily see it

dynamics the way in which a particular situation develops

dystopian relating to an imagined state or society where life can be unjust and hard

enough having the amount needed or as much as required

extent how large, important or serious a situation is

fluently the ability to speak a language easily and well

flyer a small sheet of paper advertising a product or event

goal objective; the result someone hopes to achieve

hand out to give something to different people in a group

healthy having good health; unlikely to become sick

hobby an activity people do in their free time for pleasure

impartially in a way that treats all sides equally

knowledge information and skills obtained through experience or education

leadership the state of being the leader

leisure activities that people do to relax in their free time

lifestyle a person's way of living

match a sports event where athletes or teams compete against each other

pollster a person who interviews someone else for research about a particular topic

pretend to act in a way so that people believe something that is not true

record to keep information by writing it down

role the position assumed by a person in a situation or presentation

sleepy feeling tired and in need of sleep

spread to share information about something

staff the workers of a company or organization

trampoline a piece of equipment used for jumping up and down for exercise or sport

treasurer a person who is responsible for managing an organization's money

turn out to have a particular result

update to add the most recent information

vacant unoccupied; available

UNIT 8

affordable not expensive for ordinary people

challenge an invitation for someone to participate in a competition or complete a task

classify to organize something into categories

cloud a gray or white visible mass of small drops of water in the sky

daily done every day

deadline the limit time or day for something to be done

the dishes all the plates, glasses and cutlery that have been used during a meal

distinguish to notice the differences between things or people

erupt when a volcano ejects lava, ashes and rocks

fixed not changing

flat having a surface that is smooth and uniform

follower a person who chooses to receive someone's updates on social media

grade a mark (represented by a number or letter) to assess students' performance in school

meal an occasion when someone eats at a specific time

plane a flying vehicle with two wings and at least one engine

prompt a series of directions or words to guide somebody's actions

revolve to move around a central point

rise to move upwards

schedule a plan listing all the activities to be done and at what time they must be done

shoot to record a video or take photographs

skit a short piece of humorous writing or performance

slot a space in which something can be fit

stuck unable to move or to be moved from a certain place or position

subway a train that usually travels underground

timeline a line that represents a period of time and shows important events that took place during it

upstairs on a higher level of a building

wash to clean with water and soap

weekly done every week; happening once a week

WORKBOOK 1

Name: Ítalo Matheus Alencar Santana Class: 6º A

1 Read the social media profile and write the headings in the correct place.

Birthday E-mail Last Name
Name Nationality Username

Home | Profile | Friends | Inbox

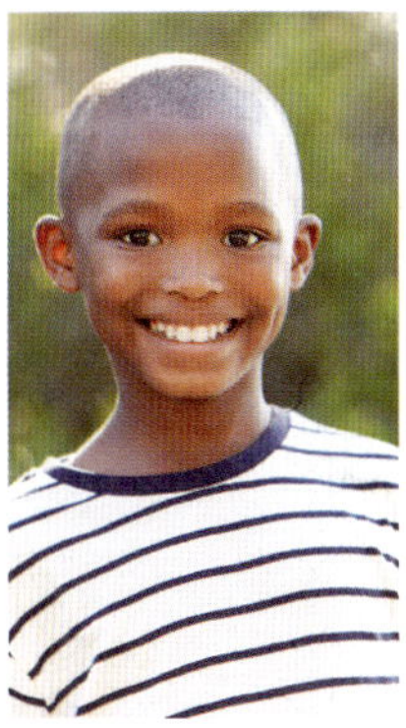

Personal Information

1 Username
superakin

2 Name
Akin

3 Last name
Darego

4 E-mail
akin10.darego@tweenmail.com

5 Nationality
Nigerian

6 Birthday
July 10, 2004

About Me

I'm from Abuja, the capital of Nigeria. I love video games and online videos. My favorite gaming vlogger is RockyCatTheGamer. He's pretty cool.

2 Read the text in activity 1 again and answer the questions about Akin.

1 What is Akin's last name?
Darego

2 What is his nationality?
He's Nigerian

3 What is his e-mail?
akin10darego@tweenmail.com

4 What does he like?
He's like video games and online videos

5 Who is his favorite gaming vlogger?
Is RockyCat

3 Circle the countries, months and nationalities in the word search. Then write the words under the correct categories.

X	H	J	C	V	B	J	M	N	M
Z	A	U	S	T	R	A	L	I	A
Q	I	L	I	H	P	P	K	G	Y
H	T	Y	N	E	L	A	O	E	G
K	I	Q	D	M	K	N	C	R	H
L	A	S	I	S	J	E	T	I	T
M	N	X	A	V	B	S	O	A	D
A	U	G	U	S	T	E	B	R	X
G	E	R	M	A	N	B	E	D	W
C	X	J	A	N	U	A	R	Y	Z

Countries
1 Nigeria
2 India
3 Australia

Nationalities
1 Japanese
2 Haitian
3 German

Months
1 Auguste
2 January
3 July
4 May
5 October

4 Underline the name of the country or nationality to complete the sentence correctly.

1 Anime is a **Japanese** / **Japan** animation.
2 I think Ms. Black is from **English** / **England**.
3 Jeff is **Scottish** / **Scotland**, right?
4 My mother's family is from **Indian** / **India**.
5 My grandmother is **German** / **Germany**.

5 Complete the sentences with the contracted form of the verb to be.

1 He ______ American.
2 They ______ Australian.
3 I ______ a student.
4 We ______ brothers.
5 She ______ from Germany.
6 You ______ the English teacher, right?

6 Complete the text about Aiko with *am*, *is* or *are*.

Hey, everyone!
My name (1) ______ Aiko. I (2) ______ 13 years old and my birthday (3) ______ in April. I (4) ______ from Japan. Here (5) ______ three facts about me. Fact number 1: I (6) ______ biracial. My father (7) ______ Japanese and my mother (8) ______ from the United States. Fact number 2: I have two brothers. Their names (9) ______ Daido and Maki. Fact number 3: I have a robot dog. Its name (10) ______ Hana-chan and it (11) ______ so cute!

7 Read the text about Aiko again and check the correct statements.

1 ☐ Aiko is 12.
2 ☐ Her birthday is in April.
3 ☐ Her father is Japanese.
4 ☐ Her mother is Japanese too.
5 ☐ Her brothers' names are Daido and Maki.
6 ☐ She has a robot cat.

8 Separate the words to make sentences. Then write these sentences using the correct punctuation and capitalization.

1 thisiscarterhesmybestfriend
______
2 himynamessofia
______
3 thatsright
______
4 hicarter
______
5 hisofiahurryupguyswerelate
______
6 sofiayoureamericanright
______
7 heyimlucas
______

9 Use the sentences from activity 8 to write a dialogue.

Lucas: ______
Sofia: ______
Lucas: ______
Sofia: ______
Lucas: ______
Sofia: ______
Carter: ______

10 Write a paragraph about yourself. Mention the topics below.

- name
- nationality
- age
- birthday
- e-mail
- favorite things

Hello! I'm ______

Extension

Name: Julia Franco Amado Class: 6º C

1 Look at Megan's family tree and complete the sentences.

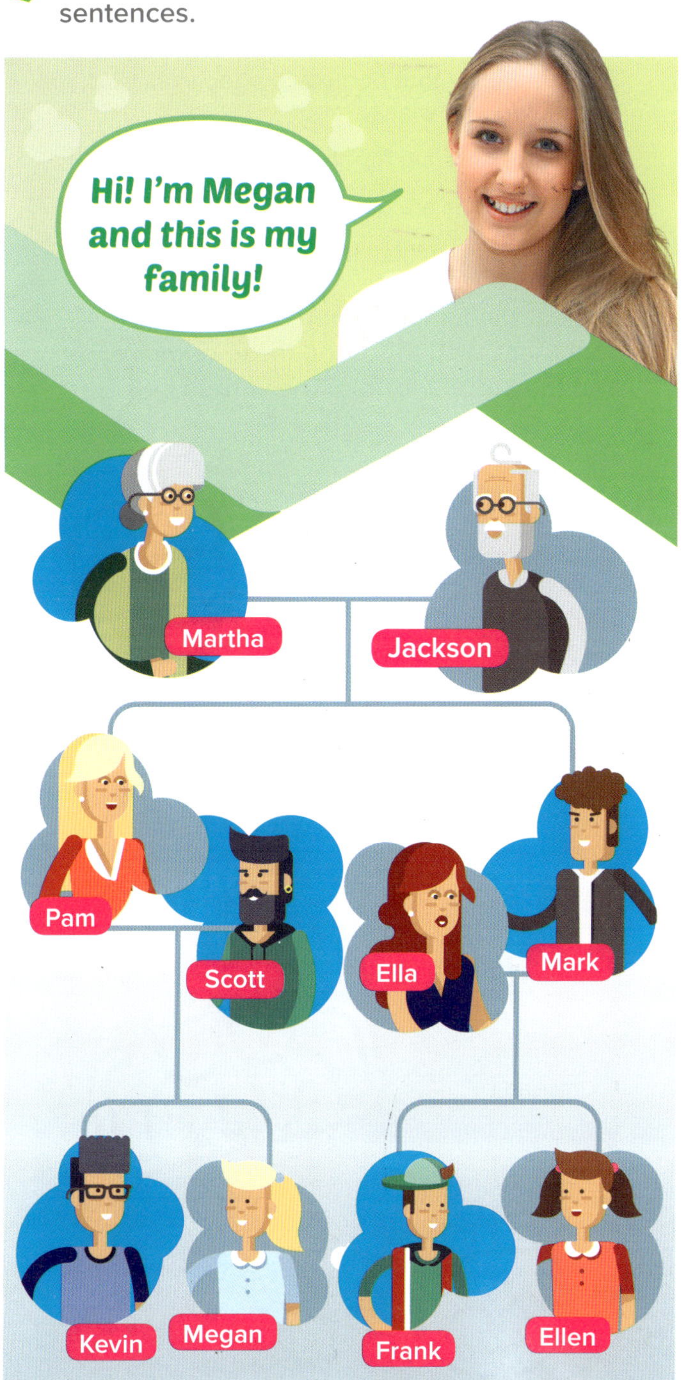

1 Scott is my father.
2 Ella is my aunt.
3 Frank and Ellen are my cousins.
4 Pam is my mother.
5 Jackson is my grand father.
6 Mark is my imcle.
7 Martha is my grand mother.
8 Kevin is my brother.

2 Read the text and check the correct answers.

1 Where is this text published?
- a ☐ In a magazine.
- b ☐ In a newspaper.
- c ☒ On social media.
- d ☐ In a photo album.

2 The author uses emojis to...
- a ☒ illustrate what he/she said.
- b ☐ substitute words in the text.
- c ☐ add new ideas to the text.
- d ☐ send a secret message to the reader.

3 Who is the author of the text?
- a ☐ The woman on the right.
- b ☒ The woman on the left.
- c ☐ The man holding the boy.
- d ☐ The young girl.

3 Find the mistakes in the sentences. Then rewrite the sentences correcting these mistakes.

1 You is tired? ____________
2 Is we at school? ____________
3 It am lunchtime? ____________
4 Your mom are a student? ____________
5 Are it sunny today? ____________
6 Your school am big? ____________

4 Answer the questions from activity 3 about yourself. Use short answers.

1 ____________
2 ____________
3 ____________
4 ____________
5 ____________
6 ____________

5 Look at the images. Then write sentences using the prompts below and the correct form of the verb *to be*.

1

he / sad

He is sad.

2

she / at school

3

they / friends

4

he / our teacher

5

they / dentists

6 Circle the correct options to complete the sentences.

1 I love **those** / **that** picture on the wall.
2 Come here and look at **these** / **this** messages from my family.
3 I need **this** / **that** book on the top shelf. Can you get it for me, please?
4 **This** / **Those** are my shoes by the door.
5 **These** / **This** are my pens. Where are yours?
6 Can you hold **this** / **those** book for me, please?

7 Look at the images. Then complete the sentences with *this*, *that*, *these* or *those* and the correct form of the verb *to be*.

1
____________ a hamburger.

2

____________ my mom's bike.

3
____________ my pets, Mimi and Lili.

4

____________ my baby sister, Barbara.

5
____________ my tennis trophies.

Extension

Name:

Class: 6º A

1 Complete the posters with the correct form of *there to be*.

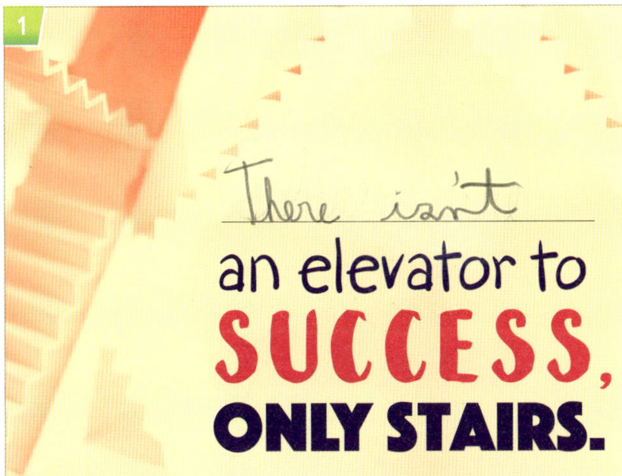

2 Match the posters in activity 1 to their message.

a [2] You should eat something.
b [3] Pay attention to the good things in life.
c [1] You have to work hard to be successful.

3 Complete the crossword and answer the question.

1 STAPLER
2 PENCIL CASE
3 PAINTBRUSH
4 NOTEBOOK
5 WHITEBOARD
6 GLUE STICK

What's the secret word? SCHOOL

4 Look at the image and complete the sentences using the prepositions from the box.

behind | between | in | in front of | next to | on

1 The laptop is <u>on</u> the table.
2 The laptop is <u>between</u> the notebook and the book.
3 The pens are <u>in</u> the pencil holder.
4 The book is <u>next to</u> the laptop.
5 The pencil holder is <u>in front of</u> the laptop.
6 The girl is <u>beching</u> the desk.

5 In which lesson do you use...

a a microscope? ____

b maps or a globe? ____

c a calculator? ____

d paint and paintbrushes? ____

e a dictionary? ____

f sports equipment? ____

6 Look at the images and name the school facilities.

1

____

2

____

3

____

4

____

5

____

6

____

7 Complete the sentences about your school. Write *there is*, *there isn't*, *there are* or *there aren't*.

1 ____ many classrooms.

2 ____ a cafeteria.

3 ____ a library.

4 ____ many students.

5 ____ a Science lab.

6 ____ Music teachers.

8 Fill in the blanks with *a*, *an* or nothing (–).

1 There isn't ____ library in my school.

2 Can you lend me ____ eraser?

3 There are ____ new desks in my classroom.

4 There's ____ auditorium in my school.

5 There are ____ pens in my pencil case.

9 Complete the text using the words from the box.

awesome classrooms grade lab large Physical Education subject swimming pool

I'm Ella Boyce. I'm in the 6th ____ and I study at Memorial Middle School. It's a ____ school with lots of facilities. There are 20 comfortable ____. There's a new gym. We have ____ classes there. There's an Olympic-size ____ too. My favorite ____ is Science. I love doing experiments in the ____. My school is ____. The only thing I don't like is the auditorium. It's very small.

10 Read the text in activity 9 again and answer the questions.

1 Is there a gym in Ella's school?

____

2 Is there a swimming pool?

____

3 Is there a large auditorium?

____

11 Write a paragraph about your school.

____

____

Extension

WORKBOOK 4

Name: ______ Class: ______

1 Read the comic strip and answer the questions.

1 In which room of the house are Charlie and Sally? ______

2 Is that Charlie's or Sally's room? ______

2 Read the comic strip in activity 1 again and circle the correct options.

1 "This is it" means **"It's time!"** / **"Let's eat!"** in the first panel.

2 The situation in the comic strip happens **in the morning** / **at night**.

3 Sally is **happy** / **nervous** about the first day of school.

4 Charlie is **confused** / **positive** about Sally's emotions.

3 Look at the image of the bedroom and check the items you see.

a ☐ bed
b ☐ chair
c ☐ lamp
d ☐ mirror
e ☐ computer
f ☐ nightstand
g ☐ desk
h ☐ wardrobe
i ☐ dresser
j ☐ TV

4 Look at the images and names and write sentences about where these people are.

1

Wade

Wade is in the bedroom.

2

Sophia

______

3

Mr. O'Neill Baxter

______

4

the Warrens

______

5

Piper

______

6

Panko

______

5 Order the words to make sentences.

1 is / Naomi / lamp / 's / yellow / .

____

2 new / 's / the / children / aren't / pens / .

____

3 bathroom / 's / big / Sylvia / is / .

____

4 husbands / my / are / ' / tall / sisters / .

____

5 there / 's / desk / a computer / on / is / Katy / ?

____

6 Look at the images and circle the correct possessive adjectives.

1

We give **her** / **our** teacher flowers at the end of the school year.

2

All my friends are happy with **its** / **their** presents.

3

Her / **His** grandpa lives in a big house.

4

The dog is under the bed. I can see **its** / **your** nose.

5

This is **his** / **my** best friend. **His** / **Your** name is Jacob.

7 Read the text and complete it with the words from the box.

's (2x) are he her his (3x) house I
is isn't my (2x) our yard

My name's Charlie Brown. I live in a small (1)______ with my parents and (2)______ little sister Sally. Sally (3)______ favorite colors (4)______ blue and pink and (5)______ best friend (6)______ name is Eudora. I have a dog, (7)______ name (8)______ Snoopy. (9)______ lives in a doghouse in the (10)______ and he spends a lot of time with (11)______ best friend, a yellow bird named Woodstock. (12)______ friends Schroeder, Linus and (13)______ sister, Lucy, are in the same baseball team. (14)______ like baseball very much, but (15)______ team (16)______ very good.

8 Do you have anything in common with Charlie Brown? Write two sentences about similarities or differences between the two of you.

My sister's favorite colors are blue and pink too. /
My sister's favorite colors aren't blue and pink.

____

____

9 Read the text in activity 7 again and write a similar paragraph about you.

____

____

____

____

____

Extension

WORKBOOK 5

Name: Ítalo Matheus Alencar Santana Class: 6º A

1 Read the chats. Which one is about…

a [ ] a party?
b [ ] a movie?
c [ ] a game?
d [ ] a school test?

1

MELISSA: It's almost time!
CINDY: I'm nervous too! But I'm sure we're gonna win!
MELISSA: I'm ready to go, OK?
CINDY: Great! Dad's getting ready and then we'll pick you up to go to the stadium.
MELISSA: Deal!

2

DAN: Hey! I'm watching a great show on TV. Wanna come here and join me?
JENNY: I'd love to, but I can't. I'm studying for the Geography test.
DAN: What Geography test???
JENNY: The one we have tomorrow…
DAN: THE GEOGRAPHY TEST! Gotta go, have to study!!!

3

CARLA: Are we on for today?
JOHN: Yeah, can't wait! Time to celebrate! See you at 4.
CARLA:

4

SUE: Hey! U busy?
FRANK: Not really. Actually kinda bored.
SUE: I'm dying to watch that new comedy. Wanna join me?
FRANK: Sure! Meet you at your house in 10 minutes so we can go together?
SUE: Awesome!

2 Read the chats in activity 1 again. Then read the statements about them and check the correct column.

		True	False
1	Melissa and Cindy will go to a tennis match.	[ ]	[ ]
2	Cindy's father will take her and Melissa to a sports event.	[ ]	[ ]
3	Dan is studying and texting Jenny.	[ ]	[ ]
4	Jenny reminds Dan that they have a test the following day.	[ ]	[ ]
5	John is excited about a party.	[ ]	[ ]
6	Sue is bored.	[ ]	[ ]
7	Frank and Sue want to watch a horror movie.	[ ]	[ ]

3 What time is it? Look and write.

1 

It's eleven nineteen a.m.

2 

3 

4 

5 

6 

4 Match the sentences to form dialogues.

1 **A:** Let's go to the mall!
2 **A:** I'm going to the supermarket.
3 **A:** I'm sad.
4 **A:** Let's visit grandma and grandpa today!
5 **A:** I'm hungry.

a [ ] **B:** Let's go together. I need to buy bread and milk.
b [ ] **B:** Let's go to that new restaurant down the street.
c [ ] **B:** Sure! I miss them!
d [ ] **B:** Let's get together with our friends and have some fun.
e [ ] **B:** Great idea! I want to buy a new sweater.

5 What are they doing? Look at the images and write sentences.

1

2

3

4

5

6

6 Order the words to make sentences.

1 your / doing / are / homework / you / Math / ?

2 games / I / not / computer / am / now / playing / .

3 he / listening / music / to / is / pop / ?

4 aren't / our / we / school / bikes / to / riding / .

5 her / on / is / phone / she / the / talking / grandparents / not / to / .

6 living / books / they / are / in / reading / comic / room / the / ?

7 Read the post and complete it using the verbs in parentheses in the correct form.

hanna_h_smith FOLLOW

Time to hit the mall! I'm here with the gang and we (1) _____ (have) a wonderful time! I (2) _____ (try) on some hats and Phil (3) _____ (look) for ideas to design his own clothes. And, of course, we (4) _____ (laugh) at Dan's jokes. Claire (5) _____ (talk) on and on about herself and she (6) _____ (share) anything she wants to try on! And what about Michelle? What (7) _____ she _____ (do)? She (8) _____ (buy) the movie tickets, that's for sure, because she doesn't like to talk to people she doesn't know. Michelle = . Fred (9) _____ (sit) on a bench; he (10) _____ (do) anything, as usual. And what (11) _____ you _____ (do) right now?

8 Read the text in activity 7 again and write which of Hanna's friends can be described using the adjectives below.

1 shy _____
2 selfish _____
3 lazy _____
4 funny _____
5 creative _____

Extension

Name: ______________________ Class: ________

1 Read the sign and check the correct answer.

1 ________ internet access in this establishment.
- a ☐ There is
- b ☐ There isn't

2 The sign ________ people to make conversation.
- a ☐ encourages
- b ☐ prohibits
- c ☐ talks
- d ☐ obligates

3 The sign is possibly located in a ________.
- a ☐ bus stop
- b ☐ drugstore
- c ☐ restaurant
- d ☐ school

4 The intention of the sign is to be ________.
- a ☐ confusing
- b ☐ funny
- c ☐ sad
- d ☐ serious

2 Underline the correct option to complete each sentence.

1 The bakery is on Cuckoo Street. Walk for two blocks and **turn** / **don't turn** right.

2 **Open** / **Don't open** your books to page 10 and do activity 2 in pairs.

3 This is a pedestrian area. **Park** / **Don't park** here.

4 **Turn off** / **Don't turn off** my alarm. I need to wake up early!

5 Shh! **Keep** / **Don't keep** quiet and listen to the teacher.

3 Read the sentences that describe places and match the opposite ideas.

1 The place is very calm.

2 It's crowded.

3 This is a very noisy place.

- a ☐ There aren't many people there.
- b ☐ The place is very quiet.
- c ☐ It's a very busy place.

4 Complete the dog park rules using the affirmative or negative imperative form of the verbs in parentheses.

5 Read Ximena's text and write the words from the box in the correct places.

busy	crowded	sidewalks
stores	streets	traffic

Hello! My name is Ximena and I'm from Mexico City, in Mexico.

This is what the (1) ________ are like here. They are very (2) ________ and there is a lot of (3) ________ ! The (4) ________ aren't very large in most of the neighborhoods.

That's the historic center. It's always very (5) ________ because there are a lot of popular (6) ________ there.

6 Answer the questions about your neighborhood.

1 Is there graffiti in your neighborhood?

____

2 Are there traffic signs in your street?

____

3 Are there large sidewalks on your street?

____

4 Is there a movie theater in your neighborhood?

____

5 How many drugstores are there in your neighborhood?

____

6 How many bakeries are there in your neighborhood?

____

7 Write signs for the places below.

1 a museum

2 a movie theater

3 a drugstore

Extension

 Name: ______ Class: ______

1 Read the blog post and complete it with the appropriate verbs in the affirmative or negative forms.

www.richmond.com.br

Life of a Teenager

Search this blog

Recent Posts | Blog Archive | About Me | Contact

April 1, 2019

Hi, everyone, and welcome to my blog.

I'm Mason. I'm 13 years old and I (1) ______ in San Francisco, on the west coast of the United States. I (2) ______ a dog named Scooter and he's my best buddy.

I'm very active and I (3) ______ many things in my free time. I always (4) ______ sports because it's a fun way to be healthy. I swim every day and I (5) ______ beach volleyball and beach soccer twice a week. I (6) ______ beach soccer very well, but I like it and that's what matters, isn't it? I (7) ______ surfing too!

Music is an important part of my life. I (8) ______ to different types of music, but I (9) ______ jazz very much. I (10) ______ singing lessons once a week.

I will be posting about sports, music and pets. Thanks for reading and I hope you enjoy the blog!

Mason

15 comments

2 What is the best title for the post in activity 1? Read and check.

a ☐ My Best Buddy

b ☐ Welcome to My Blog!

c ☐ How to Stay in Shape

3 Read Mason's post again. Which of the following statements are true according to the text?

1 This is Mason's first post on the blog.

2 Mason is not very close to his pet.

3 He plays sports so that he can have a healthy lifestyle.

4 He plays sports at the beach every day.

5 He wants to write about sports, music and pets in his next posts.

Statements ______ are true according to the text.

4 What do you do in your free time? Write a paragraph about it.

______

______

______

______

______

5 Read the interview. Then write questions beginning with the words from the box to complete it.

do (2x) | how often | what (2x) | when

Pollster: Excuse me. Can I ask you some questions about free-time activities?

Nicholas: Sure.

Pollster: (1) ______

Nicholas: Nicholas.

Pollster: How old are you?

Nicholas: I'm 17.

Pollster: (2) ______

Nicholas: I usually play baseball in my free time.

Pollster: (3) ______

Nicholas: In the afternoon, after school.

Pollster: (4) ______

Nicholas: Hobbies? Yes, I do. I have a blog.

Pollster: (5) ______

Nicholas: Yes, but I write about other sports too.

Pollster: (6) ______

Nicholas: I update it twice a week.

Pollster: Thanks for answering my questions!

Nicholas: No problem!

6 Write the words and expressions from the box under the correct category.

beach bike blogs books comics horse magazines mall motorbike movies (2x) music (2x) musical instruments (2x) park podcasts sports (2x) table tennis TV series video games videos

Go to the...	Listen to...	Play...	Read...	Ride a...	Watch...

7 Complete the questions using the simple present. Then give short answers to them.

1 A: ______ ice hockey?
B: ______ I play very well.

2 A: ______ watch TV?
B: ______ My parents prefer reading the newspaper.

3 A: ______ without you?
B: ______ My friends always invite me to hang out with them.

4 A: ______ to country music?
B: ______ But I prefer pop music.

5 A: ______ you a lot of homework for the weekend?
B: ______ But sometimes my teachers ask me to study for tests.

6 A: ______ any musical instruments?
B: ______ I play the drums.

8 Now answer the questions in activity 7 about yourself.

1 ______
2 ______
3 ______
4 ______
5 ______
6 ______

9 Read the form and write questions about Connor. Then pretend you are him and answer them.

Name: CONNOR Age: 14

Free-time Activities	Yes	No	Comments
TV		√	watch videos online
music	√		classical
team sports		√	swim
musical instruments	√		bass—very well
movies	√		with girlfriend
books		√	comics

1 A: Do you watch TV?
B: No, I don't. I watch videos online.

2 A: ______
B: ______

3 A: ______
B: ______

4 A: ______
B: ______

5 A: ______
B: ______

6 A: ______
B: ______

10 Rewrite the sentences adding the adverbs of frequency in the correct position.

1 My sister is sleepy after lunch. (usually)
______

2 We play soccer in the park. (sometimes)
______

3 They go to the beach on Sundays. (often)
______

4 I am late for school. (never)
______

11 Write sentences about what you do in your free time. Use the words in parentheses.

1 (always) ______
2 (usually) ______
3 (often) ______
4 (sometimes) ______
5 (never) ______

Extension